"Patricia DeYoung has given us a brave and honest book, a work of psychoanalysis without jargon, a challenge to learn about and converse with our own chronic and acute shame. Her personal stories make this book hard to put down. It is a significant gift and deserves a wide and fearless readership."

Donna Orange, PhD, PsyD, author of *Nourishing the Inner Life of Clinicians and Humanitarians* and *Psychoanalysis, History, and Radical Ethics: Learning to Hear*

"In this book, Patricia DeYoung, a psychotherapist and author who learned long ago that shame is the elephant in the room, explores the role of parental and cultural shaming in her childhood. She is honest about its potent effects yet merciful towards its purveyors, herself included. She understands that shaming can become a family custom, cascading down generations in ways that trap and injure both children and parents. Perhaps most importantly, DeYoung shows how we can light the exit from this ruinous cycle by being kind."

Martha Sweezy, author of *Internal Family Systems Therapy for Shame and Guilt*

Shame and Grace

Shame silences our stories, crushes our spirits, and cuts us off from our hearts. How can we give voice to what has happened? Could we fall apart into suffering that would heal us? Might we honour desires we've disowned for a lifetime? How do we gather up our battered parts of self with tenderness? Could grief and love restore our hearts to us?

Having written groundbreaking theory about the developmental genesis of chronic shame and its treatment in relational psychotherapy, Patricia DeYoung returns to speak from her heart about what it's like to inhabit a life of shame. In six essays, she writes of the essential impasses of chronic shame: silence, dissociation, isolation, the abolition of desire, the imposition of right and wrong, and ending life without meaning. Each impasse deserves a story.

DeYoung's stories of an ordinary life start with getting born and end with getting old. They open up crucial questions: Does the shame we suffer mean we're as worthless as we feel, marking miles on a hard road to despair? Or does the longing beneath our shame mean we may hope for true connection and a chance at grace? Her essays privilege our longing and the difficult but powerful grace of being real and being-with.

In this book, shame theory meets memoir and meditation. Therapists, patients, and self-reflective readers from many walks of life will be moved and changed by time spent with this master clinician, thoughtful mentor, and fellow traveler.

Patricia A. DeYoung, MSW, PhD, is a psychotherapist and clinical supervisor • in Toronto.

PATRICIA A. DEYOUNG

Shame and Grace
Six Essays on Falling Apart
and Becoming Whole Again

Routledge
Taylor & Francis Group

NEW YORK AND LONDON

Designed cover image: ©Sanghwan Kim Getty Images

First published 2025
by Routledge
605 Third Avenue, New York, NY 10158

and by Routledge
4 Park Square, Milton Park, Abingdon, Oxon, OX14 4RN

Routledge is an imprint of the Taylor & Francis Group, an informa business

© 2025 Patricia A. DeYoung

Library of Congress Cataloging-in-Publication Data
Names: DeYoung, Patricia A., 1953- author.
Title: Shame and grace: six essays on falling apart and becoming whole again /
Patricia A. DeYoung.
Description: New York, NY: Routledge, 2025. | Includes bibliographical references and index. |
Identifiers: LCCN 2024018954 (print) | LCCN 2024018955 (ebook) |
ISBN 9781032804958 (hardback) | ISBN 9781032804934 (paperback) |
ISBN 9781003499121 (ebook)
Subjects: LCSH: Shame.
Classification: LCC BF575.S45 D49 2025 (print) | LCC BF575.S45 (ebook) |
DDC 152.4/4--dc23/eng/20240531
LC record available at https://lccn.loc.gov/2024018954
LC ebook record available at https://lccn.loc.gov/2024018955

ISBN: 978-1-032-80495-8 (hbk)
ISBN: 978-1-032-80493-4 (pbk)
ISBN: 978-1-003-49912-1 (ebk)

DOI: 10.4324/9781003499121

Typeset in Joanna
by codeMantra

In loving memory of Mary
and with thanks to Nigel and Jean
for grace embodied

Contents

Acknowledgements

I've been fortunate time and again in the kindness of colleagues, friends, and family members who've been willing to read what I write and tell me what works and what doesn't. This time it was a big ask, not because this is a big book, but because it's an unusual and personal book. This time I needed to ask family members whose memories overlap with mine: "Can you live with this?" Across the board, and in spite of the pain it stirred up for some, they said it was my story to tell. I want to thank them here – my siblings Lynn and Jim, my adult kids Adriel, Rowan, and Jason, their dad Nigel and his wife Jean, and Mary's daughter Madeleine. The generosity of their responses and their trust in my intentions gave me the space I needed to write, ponder, and re-write.

But first, I needed to know whether the writing was worth even my own time. Before finishing a first draft, I shared my work in progress with Bonnie Simpson, David Schatzky, and Pat Archer, friends and colleagues who have been in on my shame theory from the beginning, with whom I have shared hundreds of hours of peer clinical supervision, and who know from the inside how writing works. Most importantly, they know me and love me – and won't lie to me.

Bonnie told me whenever the writing touched and moved her. "I just loved it," was all she could say about one essay one day – and I believed her. It's what I most needed to hear. David told me the writing was excellent, but maybe I should cut out the theory part and just write memoir. Or better still, a novel, so that I wouldn't make myself so vulnerable. A month or two later, he read the essays again and decided that their fusion works, and also that a certain kind of vulnerability is just the way I roll, and it works too. He passed the essays on to his partner Karen Essex, another writerly minded friend and experienced therapist, and she gave me a bonus vote of confidence.

Pat Archer wrote me an email to say she was liking Essay One, and could her partner Amy read the essays too? I was pleased to say yes. Not many weeks later, when it became clear that the essays would be published, I remembered that before her recent retirement, Amy Zierler had been a professional editor. I asked if she would be willing to come out of retirement to edit my manuscript. I was more than pleased when she said yes. The combination of Pat, with her insider knowledge of me and the theory, and Amy, with her intelligent layperson's interest and editorial skill, was priceless. I was so lucky to have an editor who could understand in mind and heart exactly what I was trying to do and then help me do it far better than I would have done on my own.

In short, it was a small circle of collegial support this time, and it was also just what I needed. I'm grateful that on the strength of a 250-word back-cover kind of blurb I wrote about the essays, Anna Moore, my Routledge editor (with her team), said to go for it, no further questions asked. I'm glad I did – and that I didn't go it alone. It's good to have company, too, as I wait to hear how this uncommon little book lands with readers.

Pat DeYoung
Midland and Toronto, Ontario
March, 2024

Essay One

Putting your thoughts into writing says that they matter, even thoughts about yourself. When I was eleven, I wrote an autobiography about what had happened to me and my family in each of the thirteen places I had lived in since I was born. It was for me, not for school. I wrote in neat cursive on just one side of twenty-six sheets of lined paper, in pencil so I could erase mistakes. My round blue pencil sharpener made a sharp point that didn't break, and I had a clean rubber eraser that left no smudges. I wrote when I was in the basement after supper and they thought I was doing homework. Before I would write something new, I would always read what I had already written. When it was finished, I liked holding the weight of the pages in my hands and knowing exactly what all the words said. I kept it in my bottom drawer – under hand-me-down sweaters from my cousin, the tight, fluffy ones that I never wore unless I had to.

The grey and white kitten sweater was the worst, but for a special day my mother liked it best, to go with the black wool skirt that was too tight because my waist wasn't slim like my cousin's. It buttoned in the back where I couldn't reach it. Once when my mom had buttoned it, she turned me toward the mirror and pulled the kitten sweater a little more tightly from behind. "Look," she said. "That's why we need to get you a bra." I quickly looked away from the little nubs poking out, feeling a scared kind of sick. It was happening and there was nothing I could do about it.

One day my autobiography was in my second drawer, so I knew my mom had found it. I folded it up, wrapped it in a grocery bag, and stood on a chair to put the package on the top shelf of my closet, in the back corner. I didn't have to read it to know what it said, but I would always know where to find it. When we moved to Mississippi, I threw it away, since I was older then and it was out of date. I was glad that my mom had never mentioned it to me.

DOI: 10.4324/9781003499121-1

I think I showed her my ninth-grade paper on Jonathan Edwards, who was born on my birthday 250 years before I was born. He was the Puritan preacher of the famous sermon, "Sinners in the Hands of an Angry God." I would have shown it to her after I got the grade on it. I think she just looked at the grade; it would have been an A. That's what I always got because writing was easy for me.

I wrote it to prove that predestination made more sense than free will. A library book on Jonathan Edwards talked about the British empiricists of his day, and so I quoted them to show that it isn't just a religious idea that people's wills aren't free; it has philosophical arguments behind it. People think they are choosing, but they are actually just reacting to all the forces that have formed them and come at them every day. You could think of God as the Being behind all those forces that they might never even notice. By then, I was a Presbyterian (sort of) in a school full of Baptists and Methodists who believed in free will. A White Presbyterian in a school full of White Baptists and Methodists. I didn't think about the Whiteness then. It seemed we weren't supposed to pay attention to the difference between Black and White in Mississippi.

My father preached in White Presbyterian churches, but he wasn't a real Presbyterian either. He was Dutch, from Iowa, and Christian Reformed ("CRC"). So that's what I really was, too. But as CRC, he believed in predestination and an angry God even more strongly than Southern Presbyterians did. He typed his sermons on half sheets of paper pre-folded into thin booklets that could be carried inside a Bible. He could turn the pages of the booklet as he got through his points, usually three, sometimes starting with the same letter: Praise, Prayer, and Purity, for example. That would be a sermon on Christian Living. Like all of them, it would be built on a Bible text.

In Omaha, Nebraska, I listened to my father preach every Sunday, morning and evening. In Mississippi, he didn't have a church. He had been called by a CRC church in Iowa to be a kind of missionary: a professor in a new Reformed seminary. (Presbyterians could also be "Reformed," an adjective with specific theological meanings, not to be confused with the Reformed or Christian Reformed Churches, denominations, thus collective nouns.) Sunday mornings he travelled to Presbyterian churches across the Mississippi countryside to make some extra money preaching. Money was tight in our family. He used his booklets of Omaha sermons, all neatly filed and ready to repeat. It seems the country Presbyterians were impressed by a preacher who was also a professor.

Sunday mornings his wife and six kids went to the local Presbyterian church without him. As the oldest kid, I helped get the little ones dressed and out the door in time for Sunday School before church, and then I kept the lid on their cut-loose craziness when we had hot dogs with ketchup and mustard for our Dad-free lunch after church. My mother would mention the failings of the sermon we had just heard: not based on the Biblical text, not theologically Reformed, just stories and platitudes. I would know what she meant; I, too, paid critical attention to the sermons from my seat in the choir pews behind the pulpit.

Years later, I learned that this was a Dutch CRC tradition: Roast Preacher for Sunday dinner. Ours was thin fast food – like the hot dogs. On the rare Sundays when Dad was home, we had pot roast with potatoes and vegetables. He wouldn't say anything about the other man's sermon, but he wouldn't contradict my mom or ask her to be quiet either. I could tell that she felt intelligent and important when she talked about sermons. Her dad had been a preacher too. As a woman, she would not be allowed to preach, but she could certainly tell a good sermon from a bad one. I saw that a woman could be smart about religion, even if she could never speak in church. She could understand the concepts and how they mattered as well as anyone could.

I understood that Calvinism was the system of doctrine behind both the Scottish Presbyterian and the Dutch Reformed traditions, and that it was all about the Word of God. "In the beginning was the Word, and the Word was with God, and the Word was God." I could recite those mysterious first words of the Gospel according to John and keep going for a verse or two. God's words called all of creation into being, the Bible is the Word of God, and so is Jesus – God's Word with us. At the centre of life is church, and at the front and centre of church – of every true church – is the pulpit from which the Word of God is to be proclaimed. This was the story that structured my childhood, the context in which my adolescent and young adult self knew how to matter.

And yes, that story effectively banished the shame of the other story. I was going to say, "of the real story," but who's to know what the real story is. Stories become real not as they are preached, but as they are lived, and we don't always know what we're living. Actually, it's a mash-up: we live what we know and what we don't know all at the same time.

Maybe you're thinking that the other story is something sordid and grotesque, sexual abuse, perhaps a cult. Yes, I have heard about those ugly undersides of religiosity; I'm a psychotherapist. But no, what also shaped my life but couldn't be discussed was ordinary: destructive relationships and emotional wounds; everyday intensities of longing, loss, envy, and despair; broken hearts and lonely souls. The daily struggle against bad odds was just a given: grandparents immigrating to homesteads on rocky northern Michigan soil (but there was Dutch community there, a church); grandparents immigrating to Chicago and then on by train to Iowa, where the farmland was rich, but they would never own an acre of it (but there was Dutch community there, a church).

In Iowa, a baby girl died of the Spanish flu, and my grandmother was never the same after, even though she gave the next little girl the dead baby's name. Or maybe she was always the same, before and after, and that was just the story they told, one of those stories that shouldn't be told when children might be listening. I was always listening. And my mother was a quiet purveyor of slightly salacious half-secrets, subtle disgust evident in a certain set of her mouth and a faint shake of her head.

One way or another, I came to know that my father was a late surprise baby (in the summer of 1931, born into the teeth of the Depression) and that when his sisters, who had left home early to marry, came back to the farm to visit, they would have to clean him up and feed him properly. But if they tried to take him away from his mother for even a few minutes, he would scream for her. This was still a mystery to them decades later, strange enough to mention to my mother. It's not strange to me, but then I'm a therapist, and I know about traumatic attachment, how children cling to the very people who neglect or abuse them because it's all they've got in a dangerous world.

I know that the Iowa grandmother went you-might-say-crazy with the menopause, and once went after her husband with a butcher knife.

My father had to stop her to save his dad. I don't know if she had murder on her mind, but my father wouldn't have known that either, one way or the other, when he was sixteen. When she was an old lady living alone, she slept with a knife under her pillow. They say she often threatened to kill herself, but I don't think she ever tried to.

When we went to visit, Grandma called me Patsy, which wasn't really my name, and she always hugged me so hard into her big squishy chest that I could hardly breathe. Grandma did her religion hard, too: Lots of church-going and reading of the Bible and devotional booklets. No swearing, smoking, drinking, dancing, or playing cards. No work on Sunday, and no pool halls ever. This last rule was especially for my grandfather who had come from a rougher family than she. He never pushed back, or so the story goes.

My Grandpa worked hard on their rented farm right through the Depression years and then the War years. When they retired to town, he worked hard as the custodian of the big Reformed Church across the street from their house. My uncle the contractor built it for them – small, square, and cinderblock, but a home of their own. A framed Bible text hung in their kitchen: "I would rather be a door-keeper in the house of the Lord than to dwell in the tents of wickedness." My Grandpa didn't say much, but I knew those were supposed to be his words on the wall.

At some point, maybe after the butcher knife incident, my father decided that if he ever married, he would wear the pants in the family. But first he had to get away from the farm. He was sorry to have just missed the war, his chance to go fly a fighter plane or a bomber and blow up the enemy. How else could you get away free and clear from a mother who possessed you, her relentless anxiety shrouded in Christian piety?

You could say that you want to become a minister. And so it was that my father was allowed to finish high school and enrol in a Reformed Church junior college half an hour's drive from the farm. He could pay his own way, even buy his own '39 Chevy, because his sisters had married men who paid for his labour on their farm or their construction site. And he made some friends at school, became part of a gospel quartet that did the church circuit as special music for Sunday evening services. His friend the tenor was going out with the pianist. He set my dad up for a Fourth of July date with the pianist's sister. Both were daughters of the CRC minister of a nearby town, a minister who had recently moved to Iowa from Michigan.

Clearly the farm boy was punching above his weight with this preacher's eldest who had already finished two years of college and two years of teaching in one-room country schoolhouses to make her money for school. But she was also painfully shy and more scared of things than she let on. He was physically strong and capable – and he so badly needed someone to listen to him, believe in him. She listened, she was smart, and she could see her future as this minister's wife. He was a sensitive, brooding kind of handsome. She was slim and pretty in her pin-curled bob, pleated skirts, and twinset sweaters. The tenor and the pianist broke up. My dad and mom didn't.

In the fall, they both left Iowa for the CRC college in Michigan. It was her third year there. His CRC friends joked about the upgrade as he slid across easily from Reformed to Christian Reformed. At Christmas they were engaged. The following Christmas break, they were married, not waiting to graduate first. They were going to be careful about birth control, because he still had three years of seminary after this last year of college, and she would teach school to put him through. She was fitted for a diaphragm, and she used it, but she found the spermicide jelly too disgusting to use. I was born nine months and six days after the wedding and was brought home to a travel trailer, the housing they could afford with the money saved from summer.

Let's stop there for now, since in this story I have now entered the world of my family. This world will be shaped and driven by chronic shame, but the shame story will remain in the shadows. Its pain will not be touched by grace. If you have read other things I have written, you will know where I am going with this, seventy years after that inauspicious beginning. My mission has been to tell the story of relational chronic shame, so that its pain can be touched first of all by the grace of understanding.

———————

My book about understanding and treating chronic shame is rife with footnotes and references to neuroscientific and psychoanalytic theory. It's an academic/professional book to help therapists in their work, but scores of ordinary people – among them many off-duty therapists – have emailed me to say, "This is my story," and to ask, "Where can I find a therapist who can help me with this?" In the second edition, I finally try to come clean about the shame of being White in Mississippi in the 1960s. And the shame of being born of North American settler people, who are still erasing Indigenous Peoples in the 2020s. Those are complicated discourses. Worried about appropriating others' voices and perpetuating my White and settler privilege, I added many more references and notes.

This time my writing won't be built on notes and references, though I'll give credit where credit is due. I'm not telling anyone else's story. It's just me here, writing my thoughts on shame and life, starting with my life. I'd like to find out whether my thoughts can stand up to the power of shame and survive still standing.

The story of chronic shame is not really so complicated. It goes like this, in words that I might say to a client:

> I hear you saying that you feel there's something wrong with you, something defective deep down. Nobody knows this defective-you because you work really hard to hide it. But you're afraid it comes through anyway, and that if you're not careful, everyone will know. This worried shame feeling is a terrible thing to carry around. Even if you can keep it small and quiet, it's always there.

I pause. My client nods to let me know I'm getting it, so I go on.

> In fact, there's nothing deeply wrong with you. Your head probably knows this. But you feel wrong. Why would that be?
> I think it's because something happened to you. Over and over, when you needed loving connection, you got control or disconnection instead. You were alone with nobody to help, and everything felt bad. To make sense of things, you believed the bad was in you. I think that's what happened. Making that kind of sense, a shame kind of sense, kept you from falling apart. And it still does, mostly, but it also still feels really bad.

If the storyline fits, the client may ask, "How can therapy help me with this?" I try to give a brief but honest answer.

We'll need to explore what happened, how shame got into your system early and has never let go. Understanding what has happened can interrupt the shame process and start something new. That's our hope here. We'll talk about things that trouble you in your life now and in your memories of the past. We'll explore your thoughts and feelings with no agenda, no judgment, just with kindness and curiosity. This is the new process, and as it gets stronger, you'll start to feel respect and compassion for yourself. That will make it easier to be with other people too.

It's too much for clients to believe that a process of understanding and compassion could become stronger than the process of shame they know so well. But it matters that they hear me saying it, having hope for them. It matters that a conversation about shame has begun.

———————

To come back to our present conversation: I don't blame religion for the shame that clings to so many of its adherents. I believe that one can be devoutly religious – as a Christian, Jew, Muslim, Hindu, Sikh, Buddhist, or Other – and also be open, curious, compassionate, and trusting of self and others. I don't believe that religions themselves, even the ones that specialize in self-abnegation or repenting from sin, instil the multigenerational and personal chronic shame of which I speak.

But if chronic shame is already there in families and communities, religion can give people ostensible reasons for the shame they suffer, or give them excuses to inflict shame on others and thus escape shame themselves. Religion can be used to split a group, a nation, or the world of humanity into "us," the righteous and deserving, and "them," the disgusting and undeserving. Religion-that-divides includes religion in its broadest sense – for example, the evangelical Christian right in the United States, anti-communist in the 1950s, anti-feminist in the 1960s, anti-gay perpetually, and recently aligned with "Make America Great Again." With or without theology, this broadly based community has been powered by a visceral belief system that assigns value to some people and to other people a place of shame.

I have written more about this elsewhere.[1] Here, I'm noting the subtext of shame in the culture surrounding this young couple in October of 1953; it will inform the personal shame they carry and how they carry it. Twenty-two and twenty-three years old, they bring their baby home to a trailer and lay her in a dresser drawer just the right size for a newborn. Soon there will be a crib and a small apartment; the new mother will begin to teach kindergarten in the mornings; the new father will babysit while studying. The chosen poverty of graduate school, seven years of it, two more babies and a doctorate in Amsterdam, will not be the problem.

The problem will be simply this: relational and emotional distress will push them to the edge of falling apart, and no one will be able to speak of it. Instead, there will be group rituals of worship, repentance, and forgiveness; they will seek strength in the righteousness of God and comfort in His love. Meanwhile, the unacknowledged acid of shame will keep bubbling beneath what they can know and say, eating away at the possibilities of love between them.

With only this much story, you will understand that this young man who seeks to minister has locked away a chaos of childhood pain. You won't be surprised to hear that he will meet any threat to his shaky, shame-prone selfhood with a surge of rage. Rage momentarily strengthens his grip on his slippery sense of personal power. His rage to control chaos, to not be wrong, will hurt those he loves, his wife directly, which will amplify his shame, and then, as he sees it, she will be even more wrong for making him out to be shit and feel like shit. If she doesn't fight back, after a while he calms down. Rageful blame is his way to get his shame out and away from him, and it's her job to absorb it.

Mostly she does the job, but she can never swallow all the blame. She fights back like underdogs do, with mumbled half sentences. Nothing fiery, but just enough, we kids know. Just enough to blame him back and keep the fight going.

My brother Jim says he'd think, "Don't say that, don't go there. You know what will happen." But she would, and he would be mad at her for being stupid. I was mad at my dad for being mean. But mostly I was just dead scared of how the fights felt, more scared than the others were. Maybe that was because I had been alone with the two of them from the beginning. I was well-past four before my first brother was born.

I didn't think my mother was stupid; I thought she was weak. And this couldn't be helped; she was a woman. Now, I think she was neither stupid nor weak. She was a woman schooled in the rules of her time and place, an American, college-educated, White evangelical Christian woman, coming of age in the early 1950s. She wasn't supposed to have a voice. She was supposed to be a helpmeet, and all the more so if her man were a minister of God. Under those circumstances, she was stupid like a silent fox and also incredibly resilient. Staying with him made all the sense in the world – the world into which she had been born.

———————

My mother's father was a confident extrovert of a minister, his wife quiet and reserved. Theirs had been a romantic love story – a boy and a girl from neighbouring Michigan farms, the boy a bookish one who wrote poems to the younger girl he loved as he went off to college and seminary, his call to ministry clear. Tuberculosis interrupted, then long months in a Colorado sanitarium, with many letters between them their only link. Finally, with one lung collapsed but no longer ill, he came home to marry his bride and take her away to a climate drier and warmer than northern Michigan – first to the dry side of the Washington mountains, and then to Texas, where he, too, became Southern Presbyterian, even a revival tent preacher for a time. Eight and a half years after marrying, they would have a first child, my mother. My grandmother's health suffered, the story goes, but then she recovered and had three more children.

None of them ever became Texans. The family visited their Michigan relatives whenever they could, and as my mother neared her teens, her parents decided to bring the family home. My grandfather became principal of the Christian high school he had once attended – cringeworthy for my mother at thirteen, a new kid in this new school and her dad the principal. After she had graduated, he accepted a call to take up the ministry he had always wanted, a Christian Reformed Church, one that happened to be in a Dutch farming community in Iowa. My grandparents were a good fit there, and eventually all three of their daughters married Dutch boys from Iowa farms.

There's no visible trauma in this story, no shame of helpless victimhood for my mother to block out. What happened, then, that her presence was so very guarded and elusive? She was somehow always there, subtly intrusive, silently wanting but never saying, but she was also never there, slip-sliding away from whatever she might have said or done. I've told myself that she was just born shy and scared. But I have also trolled for pieces of a story that would help me decipher the enigma.

My mom's mom had an older brother who slowly died of diabetes before he was ten, before the discovery of insulin. This grandma was thirteen when her own mom died, and then she became the home-maker for her father on the farm. My grandpa, her prince, wouldn't come for her until she was twenty-three.

A long lifetime later and back in Michigan, the family gathered with my grandmother's closed casket the night before her funeral. A CRC Elder who was also an old family friend drew us together and spoke directly to her children: my mother, an uncle, two aunts. By then I was a mother too. I stood in this silent circle of family, a thick muffling of carpet under our feet, yellow lamplight on our sombre faces.

"I want to tell you this," the Elder said.

I know that your mother could never say that she loved you. We all know that she lost her own mother when she was just a girl. The words 'I love you' were not there for her. But from every talk I've had with her since your father died, I know that she loved each of you dearly. I hope that you always felt her love, and can still feel it – love stronger than words.

One of my aunts was crying then, but my mother wasn't.

My feelings: First, quiet shock that a man of the church could speak so plainly of human pain and love. Second, *aha!* Maybe the mystery of my mother lies hidden in her relationship with her mother.

Slowly a story has come to me, though I'll never know how true it is. Maybe there was more missing for my mother than the word "love." At twenty-three, my grandmother might have envisioned family life as she was supposed to, but what if eight years later she resented the intrusion of an actual baby? At long last she had escaped to an adult relationship where she was beloved and free. How could a baby, even a prayed-for baby, not be a spoiler in that Eden? How could she admit such feelings to herself – or to her husband! – without shame? Was she depressed, postpartum? The story I heard was about high blood pressure that somehow resolved itself. Did my grandmother's spontaneous recovery mark her slow coming around to accept, and then to embrace, the role of mother?

What happens to an infant who lives with a mother's illness or depression? Disconnection feels like rejection. What happens to a child whose mother is ambivalent about her existence? Maybe she wants to disappear, not to be seen by empty eyes. What if her father dotes on her a bit, and the sting of jealousy compounds her mother's shame, even while she makes sure, as his wife, that she still matters most to him? If the adults cannot bear to feel the force of this new triangle of need, love, and hate, the child will nevertheless absorb the anxiety and forbidden shame of it. What if, when the little girl is three, a baby brother is born who becomes the apple of his mother's eye? Soon thereafter, there's a baby sister, lively and bright, bringing a gleam to both parents' eyes. And then a few years later, there's one more baby, and now this is a big, happy family that loves children, even if the parents don't speak the word to them directly.

What becomes of that first child, the intruder, the spoiler? The mother gets over a hard time, but the child's sense of self is shaped by what has happened between them. She was born sensitive, a thin skin between herself and the world. A blankness in her mother's eyes, a stiffness in her hands, has left her untethered, ill at ease in her body, seeing herself from the outside, anxious about belonging. Anyone's gaze is a threat. She is scared of tornadoes, house-fires, loud noises, and germs, but most of all she is scared of people.

This first child is quiet and good, but she keeps her distance from people and watches them to keep herself safe. They mustn't see her watching. She learns to listen and to watch from behind her eyes, seeing what people do right or wrong, how they get what they need. She looks down on those who fail, but as one who has been supplanted, she also doesn't like winners. Her only way to win will be to marry a winner. No one, especially not she herself, is to know about her ambition and her envy, her suspicion that she will always be shortchanged, and the myriad tiny ways she will try to get something for herself anyway.

As an adult, she will live uneasily with herself, for despite these undertows of judgement and envy, every day she will sincerely try to "Trust and obey / For there's no other way / To be happy in Jesus / But to trust and obey."[2] This is the lilting chorus of a Sunday School song my mother taught me before I went to school. The storyline: When we walk with the Lord in the light of His Word, when we persist in trusting Him and obeying his Word, He abides with us and shines glory on our way.

I knew in the rhythms of daily family life what this Trust and Obey felt like. Before every meal, we bowed our heads and closed our eyes, and one of the adults spoke a conversational prayer of thanks to our Heavenly Father for immediate gifts – such as a good night's rest, or someone's safe journey home – followed by requests for blessings for ourselves and other people who needed God's care that day. There would be the essential petition: "Forgive us our sins, and keep us from sin this day." Words of gratitude for the food before us, graciously provided by the Lord, would come last, and then we could eat.

Now of course I knew that my mother, not the Lord, had made the spaghetti, but I also knew that like all good things, it came ultimately from God, beginning with the sun and rain on farmers' fields. She might even have made it ungraciously, but that wouldn't make it less a gift from God. People just did what they had to do; all the grace belonged to God.

After every meal when we had been sitting around a table, mostly Sunday dinners and weekday suppers, we also had to "read and pray" together before we could leave the table and start to clean up the dishes. My parents wanted the children to understand the reading, and so for the many years when small children were at the table, we read an illustrated children's Story Bible over and over, chapter by chapter, starting with Creation and ending with Saint Paul starting the Christian Church. Those chapters were boring, but stories of people like Joseph, Esther, and Daniel-in-the-Lion's-Den were worth waiting for. Those brave young people, portrayed with fresh faces and lithe bodies in brightly coloured robes, came to feel like family to me. They trusted and obeyed God, and God came through for them.

Whenever we had adult guests, the reading would be from a booklet of daily devotions based on scriptural texts. The closing prayer would be shorter than the one before the meal, but it would end the same: "In Jesus' name we pray, Amen." This made sense to me because I understood that Jesus had died for our sins, making it possible for God to listen to us sinners even though God hates sin. If we believed in Jesus, our sin was on Him instead.

But then sometimes the adult would say, as if talking to Jesus instead of to God, "In your name we pray, Amen." But why would you use Jesus' name to have access to Jesus? (Or were they using God's name to have access to God?) Either way it made no sense to me, though later I learned that the doctrine of the Trinity could cover it somehow: any-time you talked to God, you were actually talking to the Father, Son, and Holy Spirit, even though you could talk to them separately, too.

I think the doctrine of the Trinity was what made me nervous about Jesus. The pictures in the Story Bible made him look serious but friendly even with his beard and robes (except for the one where he was sad and exhausted, carrying his cross to be crucified). There was one picture with children gathered around looking up at him. But unlike Joseph or Esther or Daniel, he didn't feel like family to me, and I don't think it was because of the beard. I think it was because I knew that he wasn't really one of us; he was really God, and God is sitting in righteousness and judgement far above us ... and now Jesus is at God's Right Hand, ruling too. The heroes of the Bible and the rest of us believers are all in the same boat down here, trying to trust and obey God (including Jesus) who sees and knows everything from above, and who holds all the truth and all the rules for human beings.

As a child, I wasn't oblivious to the complications of being both saved and a sinner in this world down here. I saw that this was essen-tially what the church and the prayers were about: trying to trust and obey, often failing, and then asking for forgiveness and strength to do better next time. Not being able to stop sinning was the reason for needing Jesus and for being humble. Every Sunday morning, the Ten Commandments were read out, plus Jesus's summary, "Love God with all your heart, soul, and mind, and love your neighbour as yourself." Then came a time for repentance, but it was still not clear to me what the sins might be that adults were repenting of. I was never warned about specific sins that I as a child might commit. I just had the general sense that it would be anything different from being a good girl, and since I tried hard to be good and mostly succeeded, I didn't worry a lot about being a sinner.

The exception was when I was ten and Billy Graham came to town. My father was one of the many Omaha ministers recruited to meet the people who would come forward to give their lives to Christ at the end of the sermon. The organ would play and George Beverly Shea would quietly sing all the verses of a simple hymn of repentance, soulful longing woven into its hypnotic refrain. From all over the stadium, people would slowly walk forward into the music. Soon there would be streams of them, while the rest of us would sit with every head bowed and every eye closed. I felt the emotion of the moment. I had listened to the powerful preaching coming in on loudspeakers. It made me feel bad about being a sinner, and I wanted to walk forward into the sweet grace of being loved and forgiven once and for all – but I peeked and I didn't see any other kids doing that. And I somehow thought my mom, sitting next to me, wouldn't like it.

One night that week, before bedtime, I mentioned casually to my mom that I had sort of thought about going forward myself. Her voice changed to come in close and I wished I hadn't said anything. She told me that emotions shouldn't be confused with faith, and that we didn't believe that going forward to accept Jesus was a necessary part of being saved. I was already a Christian; I had been since I was baptized as a tiny baby into the family of God, and I wouldn't ever have to worry about not being saved or about having to make that decision for myself.

I doubt that the word "predestination" was spoken, but the notion, or at least the security of being on the right side of it, was in the air. I didn't understand why my father would be helping people to accept Jesus into their heart if he didn't believe it was something they needed to do. Or maybe they needed to, but we didn't? But I didn't ask about that.

I was learning to live with other things that didn't add up: How my father could preach about the love of God on Sunday morning and then on Sunday afternoon, if there were no guests for dinner, he could blow up and be mean. How my mom would brag to my aunt about her smart kids, but she told me never to be proud of being smart because God gives each of us different gifts, all worth the same. How I knew that my parents loved me, but that being alone with either one of them made me want to shrink and hide inside. I knew better than to try to make sense of these things, or even to think much about them.

Now I know that many things can be true at once, and they don't have to add up. I know that it's fine to think about them, even to write about them, without having to wrestle them into a Truth that can be in the same room as the Infallible Word of God.

I'm writing into the face of shame not to say that I know the true story of what happened in my family of origin or in the families of the parents and grandparents before us. I'm writing to say that many more things were true than the story I was told, and that the painful things people felt toward one another, did to one another, whether with intention or not, didn't have to become buried vats of caustic shame to leak down into the next generation. It all could have been done differently.

This, I believe, is true for anyone in a lifelong struggle with chronic shame: not that their personal and family story is necessarily so very horrible (though there are truly horrible stories), but that painful or horrible truth was not allowed to be known and woven into their story with grief and respect. We humans are hardwired for relationship that's brought to life through emotional connection. Thus we also have countless opportunities to inflict and to suffer emotional pain in broken and spoiled relationships. When injuries between people can't be known and tended to, the shame that's a natural part of human vulnerability becomes shame about being vulnerable. When being vulnerable has become intolerable, there's no way out of the chronic state of shame, and there's no working through the ordinary emotion of shame, either.

I don't write in hopes of erasing shame. First of all, I don't believe that the ordinary emotion of shame should be erased from the human repertoire of feeling. When we hurt others, we should feel shame – it's our impetus to take responsibility for having done harm and to make things right as best we can. Sometimes this ethical emotion can do its work, moving us toward reconnection and the repair of injury. Then understanding and trust can return to damaged relationships.

But all too often we can't bear to let shame do its work. We are too deeply afraid of being vulnerable, of feeling ashamed and owning our failures. Why is this so hard for us? That's a question for another essay. Here it's enough to note that our fear of working through healthy shame leaves lots of room for chronic shame to grow and fester.

I'm not writing in service of erasing chronic shame either, though life would be simpler without it. I think that there's meaning in the trouble that chronic shame makes for us. That's why I intend to shine light on it from all sorts of directions – to come to know our foe until our foe becomes one of us, until our rigid defensive shame might give way to allowing that we are, indeed, frail, flawed, and finite. Time will tell whether this kind of knowing will also allow us to accept contrary truths about ourselves, to care for our own and others' vulnerability, and to forgive, as we also ask to be forgiven.

These words about forgiveness seem to echo the prayers of my forebears. But they aren't an "Our Father," asking God's forgiveness. I'm saying that the love we owe is to all our fellow beings on this planet. The forgiveness we need is from them, as we forgive them in turn. We seek to treat all beings who cross our path with justice and mercy, because if we don't, there will be no justice and mercy. God, assuming there is a God, can't do it without us.

Living ethically and responsibly is hard. It's easier to confess one's sins to God and to feel forgiven, partaking in grace from above. Grace here on this earth comes by way of more difficult struggles with self and other. In these essays, I will seek the grace that eases shame, and this will be the grace I mean. Not grace from above but grace from within the fragility of our hearts, the grace of human connection on a planet scarred by greed and war, a grace shared among bodies that are born to die.

Death may be the end of each of us; short or long, this life may be all we get. It seems likely, but I don't know. Who does?

My devout forebears would tell me firmly: "Faith itself is the assurance of things we hope for, the evidence of things we cannot see." In other words, setting predestination aside for the moment, we can choose to have a faith that will in itself settle for us the key issues of our living and dying.

Well, okay. Here's what I choose to believe, not that it settles anything.

I believe that humans have always flexed their minds and bodies to make the best of where they find themselves, be it cave dwellings or space stations. Their circumstances can be dire – flood, fire, drought, disease – but dire or deadly is not evil. Evil is a matter of the human heart – of intending to do harm or of failing to recognize and prevent harm. It can start with small events of greed, hurt, and reprisal, but then harms multiply, creating powerful systems of avarice, defence, and vengeance. Good is a matter of the heart, too, an enduring, courageous intention to stop harm and to move toward systems of care instead.

I believe that forces of good and evil compete to capture the power of human invention and interaction, and when good wins, people are kind and fair to one another, however difficult the circumstances. When evil wins, people turn their creativity toward taking whatever they can for themselves and for their family, tribe, or nation, with no thought for the suffering they cause.

I believe that across millennia and continents, every human culture has known about good and evil, has developed codes of right and wrong behaviour, of honour and shame, and has told stories of higher forces or beings that infuse its ethic with luminance and power. As we've noted, almost any religion can turn out to reinforce selfish intentions and actions. I believe, however, that our stories of higher powers are born not only from our desire to protect our fearful fragility but also from our need to protect the goodness of community life. Humans are self-centred and mean-spirited, even in their religions, but humans are also thoughtful, generous, and compassionate. I am drawn to any religion whose sense of deity reinforces human goodness.

I don't believe that we have to align ourselves with deities in order to live lives of kindness and justice. Perhaps all stories of deities are nothing more than projections of human passions. Or are there realities beyond our ken to which all such stories point, but none can capture? Again, who knows? I am drawn to believe that there is indeed a force for good beyond our capacity to articulate a name for it. Is this simply because I have been brainwashed since infancy to imagine the Christian God?

I can't answer those questions. But I had a lot of time recently, as my partner lay quietly dying, to feel that she was being received into love, not taking a slow, lonely fall into nothingness. I was surprised at the strength of my feeling. For our thirty-plus years together, we didn't pray or go to church except for ritual family occasions. We were more likely to play golf on a Sunday morning. Mary didn't believe in heaven or hell outside of the heavens and hells we create for ourselves and one another. What was happening had nothing to do with what she deserved, or didn't deserve. Or, for that matter, with what I deserved or didn't. It was just there, that sense of love larger than both of us. I let myself respond to it with thought as well as feeling.

This love felt like presence, like the relationship that lasts beyond my loved one's death, real where it lives in my memory and emotion. When I talk with Mary on my walks, sharing a sunrise or a story about my day, I know she has died. Yet our love still nourishes me, telling me, for example, that it's good to write this. The worst of who we were to each other falls away as I talk with her about that, too, forgiving her and being forgiven. It seems that on her dying I was invited with her into a liminal space of being received into love, no matter where we had come from or what we had done in our lives.

I'm telling you this so that you'll understand the next part of the story. To my surprise and disbelief, I found myself, on my walks, talking to something like God as well. I said,

> I don't believe you are a 'you,' and I've got no theology for this, but I want to say that I am so very deeply grateful for the love I feel here with me, and in the trees and sky and wind.

Later I said,

> I'm only human, and it's beyond me to know how to relate to the power of love in the universe. So I'm just going to say 'you,' and we'll both know that I haven't got a better way to understand this, being a human wired for person-to-person love.

These days I talk to Mary less. That's the process of grieving. I will keep letting her go. She will slowly disappear into the love from whence she came, and I will go on without her. But I find myself still talking to the power of love in the universe. I suppose you could say that during the months of her dying and in the months after, I chose faith. But as it came to me, it seemed not a time of choosing, but a long moment of grace in which I could feel the faith I had been living for many unchurched years. Until I was alone with death and love, I could not claim it, because in the religious world that formed me, such faith is heresy; I am an unbeliever with no faith at all.

———————

With no knowledge of this process of mine, my ex-husband recently gifted me a text from his days in a United Church of Canada theological college: an introduction to process theology in the Christian tradition.[3]

A bit of backstory is in order here. Nigel and I married nearly half a century ago, fresh out of our CRC college, intent on doing family, career, and community-of-faith much better than our parents had done. I was lying to no one when I told him I loved him; I did and I do, but not the way a woman loves a man, or in my case, the way a woman loves a woman. But I had no idea how such love felt until I loved a woman. When I knew, he said I should follow my heart, and I did, but not without grief.

We had been married a decade before he decided on a career in the church. I moved out as he took his first parish. My mother said to one of my siblings that I left him because I didn't want to be a minister's wife.

Back to the main story and process theology in the Christian tradition. I won't become an amateur theologian. It's enough for me that there's a theology that imagines God as the force of love in the universe and understands evil as our investments in processes that destroy ourselves and others. In this theology, God has no power over this evil. If God had human emotion, God would be full of grief. But also never without hope, because God is about becoming, and becoming in relationship. Unable to prevent the harm humans do, God keeps on inviting us to choose processes of justice and healing, and to open ourselves up to more connection and wholeness. It's up to us which processes we choose and how we move with them.

This is what I choose to believe about God, not that it settles anything. It doesn't settle the question of God for anyone besides me because pluralism is built into the theology: there's room for the power of love to take many forms, including many names of deities and codes of ethical behaviour. Nor does it settle the question of God for me forever. I am, as I write, grasping onto something new, but then this will open into something else, something I can't imagine now, because it hasn't happened yet. It's a process.

And how many times have I said that to a psychotherapy client and to myself as we struggle together to find their path toward healing and wholeness: *It's a process.* And: *Healing comes by way of relationship.* That's one more thing that slid into place for me as I walked that windy country road in the spring and began to speak to a being I had never before imagined: This is what I do for a living – invite people into a relational process that moves toward well-being. This is what I write and teach about.

But before I saw my career through the lens of process theology, the span of my whole life had been coming back to me unbidden. One morning I stopped in my tracks. A sudden awareness took my breath away and moved me to tears: *You have been with me all this time.* All those times when I did the next thing I could imagine and it turned out to be far less than perfect, all those decisions that I can now see were driven by fear and unmet need – they were what I could do then and there, given the destructive patterns I was trying to work my way out of. The invitation to heal, to love, and to live life fully was there all that time, too, and I was always listening for it, responding as best I could.

Now I had time to look into the faces of those younger versions of myself, to put an arm around them, one by one. I told them,

It's okay. You were doing what you could with what you knew. What you did got us here, and now, going forward, there can be more healing and wholeness, maybe even joy. The process continues, and as long as we live, the power of love in the universe will give us more chances.

It's one thing to have that experience, another to write it. Writing is a stand I take. I am stepping beyond my expectations of judgement and scorn; I am inviting understanding and respect. I didn't think I could tell you how writing could stand up to shame. I wanted to be able to show you, and what has happened so far in this essay will suffice.

But there are still a few more things I would like to tell you, speaking as a fellow human being and also as a therapist who has seen and known a lot of chronic shame.

First, there's no magic in the activity of writing. It's just one way to tell the story of what happened — not the family myth of what happened, or what was supposed to happen, or what you made happen anyway and after, but what actually happened to cause you emotional pain and shame. Writing isn't the only way to tell that story. The classic way is to speak it in fifty-minute segments of conversation with a therapist who hears and draws out what you can't quite say yet. But you can speak it, instead, to your lover or your friend if that works for them and for you. You can paint or sculpt it. You can write lyrics and music and sing it out. You can dance it or beat it out on a drum: *This is me, here, knowing what happened and feeling it.*

Second, if chronic shame is what's troubling you, it's going to take you far longer to find the story you need to tell than you would imagine. That's because the mission of chronic shame is to turn the unbearable feelings of childhood into, "It's my fault. There's something wrong with me." That story is just bearable, but not shareable; compensatory stories will protect and disguise it. You will have to get through the stories where you're the martyr or the hero, winning against all odds. You will have to get past the stories that blame those who hurt you. You will have to persevere through your here-and-now stories of feeling crappy about yourself, alienated from others, exhausted with the struggle. All these stories need to be heard, but they are all still part of the shame-and-self-protection process. They are not the stories that will interrupt chronic shame and start a new process.

The stories you most need to tell are simple, but you can't tell them for real until you can feel them for real: *I wasn't seen or known. I didn't matter. I was not loved. I was not lovable.*

And if those were the stories you were living then, but they never got told, they will be the stories you are still living: *I am not seen or known. I don't matter. I am not loved. I am not lovable.* That's the unbearable layer of feeling that persists under your chronic shame, and it's so very hard to trust that going there to feel it has anything to do with healing.

In this moment, I see that although the childhood story I have just told you comes from that layer of feeling in me, I have not been direct about the feelings. I have let the story suggest and hold them. But lest you think those feelings are unspeakable, let me say this plainly. I felt annihilated in the presence of my father's rage. Nothing mattered but what he felt. I felt a shrinking emptiness in the presence of my mother's hate – for of course I was a spoiler, too, of her Eden, and the thief of my father's love. I felt ugly in the presence of her ubiquitous disgust. I felt weighed down and tied up by what they made of me in their minds, and I felt an aching lone-liness in the presence of their emotional absence. I felt terrified for their safety and my safety whenever their ongoing fight broke out, even as I disappeared. In short, I felt that I was not seen or known, that I was not loved or lovable, and that I didn't matter. Sometimes, on bad days, I still feel some of that.

None of that is too hard to say now, but I was a long time getting to it. So it goes.

The third thing I want to be sure to share with you is this: When this hidden layer of story becomes a crucible of alien anguish for you, know that this intensity of pain will pass. This is not all of who you are or will be. This story is a deeply significant part of your life, but not the only truth. It doesn't invalidate all your other stories; it links with them into a larger whole. This work we do with chronic shame is about integration, not about splitting things up all over again into true or false, right or wrong, saints or monsters.

My mother who didn't much like me (or that's what I felt) walked with me into the North Sea off Scheveningen beach, pretending to be as immune to cold water as I was. We walked to where the waves stopped rolling in, almost over my head, because she wanted to teach me to swim. Floating came first, and we needed still water for that. I remember her hands under my shoulders as she told me to relax, to lay my head back into the water. Slowly, slowly I came to feel the water holding me up, and then her hands were just there lightly, for safety.

My mother read all of the Laura Ingalls Wilder *Little House* books to me when deep woods and wide-open prairies were far away on the other side of the ocean. She helped me learn to ride her big steel Dutch bike on grassy paths in the North Sea dunes. In later years, she showed me how to beat an egg with a fork, her wrist whipping quickly, and she taught me how to make spaghetti sauce with hamburger meat and Italian seasoning. She always made sure that we had a green and yellow vegetable with our meat and starch, and a piece of fruit in our lunch boxes.

When my father walked out of the therapy session in which I came out to my parents (as he left I called him a chickenshit), she stayed and let the therapist help us talk for a while. I could tell she was anxious about him – Where did he go? Was he okay? – but she stayed until the end, and she talked. But still I was surprised, twenty-five years later, when she saved a seat for me at the private family meeting that was held before my father's funeral began. It seemed she wanted me there beside her.

These days I call her Tuesdays at 12:20–1:00, a gap in my clinical day. If I'm not working, I often forget to call. She's mostly okay with that, because she's aware that she doesn't remember to call anybody; they have to call her. We talk about the weather, her health, events of our week, news about my siblings. Sometimes we drift into innocuous memories of the old days, Holland or Omaha or Mississippi, and often note the time that has passed, fifty or sixty years or more.

I can't call my dad now, but I called them both every Thursday for a year after he was diagnosed and before he died. Before I remember his dying, though, let me go back to when we were young.

My young father whose rage terrified me walked with me on that Scheveningen beach in the spring and the fall. We leaned into the wind as the gulls swooped and screamed above us. His big warm hand held my small one. We looked down at the sand for interesting stones and shells, over to the wide grey sea rolling in on foamy waves, and up at the billowing, scudding clouds.

In Nebraska, early one fall morning, I sat silently in a blind up a tree with him as we waited for deer to come by. They would have had to come close because he didn't have a gun, just a fifty-pound bow and very sharp arrows. I was cold and bored, but I kept very still. No deer came by.

My dad never shot a deer with his bow, but he did with his rifle, hunting with a friend in Wyoming. The deer came home field-dressed on the top of the car, and it became roasts, steaks, and lots of ground venison to mix with ground beef. My dad (and mom) gave me a fifteen-pound bow for my eleventh birthday, and he set up a target for me on strawbales. They gave my brother a BB gun the Christmas he was almost nine and I was thirteen. Envy flooded me as he tore off the wrapping, but then I got an even better gift – my dad's twenty-two calibre lever-action Winchester from when he was a kid on the farm. He had refinished the stock for me. In the mild Mississippi winter, he took us out to stubbled corn fields and told us we were hunting (he'd shoot a rabbit with his shotgun if he could). I always kept the muzzle of my rifle down and the safety on. At The Place I learned to target-shoot tin cans on stumps.

The Place was ten acres of Mississippi woods that my parents bought because my dad, especially, needed some land, some space. We went out there on Saturdays, and my dad would cut dead trees with a chainsaw and split firewood to take home. We tried to dam a stream to make a pond. We'd roast hot dogs over a fire and have them with potato chips and Kool-Aid. My mom would keep an eye on the little kids playing their games and running free, and I would climb the tallest tree I could find that was still skinny enough so that from the top I could sway the whole tree. My dad sold The Place after I went away to college. He had learned to fly a plane, and he used the money to buy a Cessna.

When I was fifty, I built a strawbale house a hundred yards into forty-seven acres of Ontario bush, and I had a pond dug behind it. When I was fifty-eight, my parents came there to visit us, Mary and me, for the first time. This was, in fact, the first time they had come to Canada after the debacle of the coming-out session. After twenty years my father had relented, and then as soon as he stepped on the property and looked around, he understood. It was what he might have done. We built a trellis together with my power tools, and he put some woodworking flourishes into it that I wouldn't have known how to do. He privately made his peace with Mary.

Later he called me out toward the tomato garden, a quiet side of the house, because he wanted to say something to me. "I want to say I'm sorry," he said. "I'm sorry about losing twenty years ... of this ..." He wanted to say more but he couldn't.

"It's okay, Dad," I said, warding off his choked-up pain. It was too much for me. He shook his head to say it wasn't okay, so I told him more firmly, "It's okay because you're here now. That's what matters. And I'm okay with it all. Really." Which was true enough for me. But that didn't help him with his regret and strangled grief.

My parents spent time there the next fall for a week when the colours were turning, watching birds and beavers, and then we and my kids, with their spouses and children, joined them there to celebrate my sixtieth. Two and a half years later, in the spring when I had a weekend alone at the strawbale house, a call came in from Iowa in the middle of the day. It was my father. He was going into surgery and he wasn't sure he would survive it. He was calling to tell me he loved me very much, and I told him I loved him too, very much. He didn't survive the surgery, but before he went into it, he had reached out to say goodbye and I love you to each of his six children, four of them long-distance phone calls, and somehow we had all picked up.

Such are the stories that make a life: good stories right next to bad stories; stories of pain interwoven with stories of love. They don't cancel each other out. And the last thing I want to say follows on this directly: When you write to stand up to shame, don't go for the happy ending. If the bad stories don't cancel the good ones, the good ones don't cancel the bad ones either. It all belongs to you, and as you open yourself to feel it, you will become strong enough to carry it just as it is.

A happy ending would take the incident of my father's apology and have the two of us talk together about what happened with words of forgiving love. In fact, as he struggled with his emotion, the old story flamed up in me and I was as frightened as ever of the broken, shamed intensity in him and his need that I absorb his pain to save him from it. He always needed more than I or anyone could give, and yet – or therefore – his needs were unspeakable. I never went up in his plane with him because I believed (irrationally, I know) that if the two of us were alone together up there, the plane would explode.

A happy ending would celebrate the fact that after a lifetime of emotional distance my mother and I now talk for forty minutes a week. Before we say goodbye, we each say a genuine I love you, words rare in my childhood. She means well and now she tries hard to connect, but she still carries that radioactive bundle of shame, (self-)criticism, and (self-)disgust that I know so well and that threatens my cells and molecules. I find that I can't share anything with her that's close to my heart. I'm afraid that she would feel exposed and hurt to read this, and I don't want that for her. I'm sorry that shame has been such a struggle for her, too.

It's tempting to push for a happy ending, but a false integration is actually a dis-integration. If the unspoken gets put back under the wraps of a fabricated redemption, it returns to being unspeakable, and the writing does not survive the contest; shame, the great disintegrator, wins again.

If writing survives, what it knows and says just stands there. It simply is, all of it, in the face of shame.

Last week, a client was talking to me about her parents being too broken to give her what she needed. She said, "I don't think I'm angry anymore. But all of this is just so terribly sad. Isn't there something I can do?"

"No," I said. "There's nothing to be done. Nothing you can do. But feel the sadness; be with it. I think that's the only thing that helps, and it takes a while."

NOTES

1 Patricia DeYoung, "Societies of Chronic Shame," in *Understanding and Treating Chronic Shame: Healing Right Brain Relational Trauma*, 2nd ed. (New York: Routledge, 2021), 101–134.
2 John H. Sammis, *Trust and Obey and Other Songs* (Legare Street Press, reprint from public domain, 2021).
3 Marjorie Hewitt Suchocki, *God, Christ, Church: A Practical Guide to Process Theology* (New York: Crossroad, 1982). For an introduction to process theology in the Jewish tradition, see Rabbi Bradley Shavit Artson, *God of Becoming and Relationship: The Dynamic Nature of Process Theology* (Nashville, TN: Jewish Lights, 2016).

REFERENCES

Artson, Rabbi Bradley Shavit. *God of Becoming and Relationship: The Dynamic Nature of Process Theology*. Nashville, TN: Jewish Lights.

Suchocki, Marjorie Hewitt. *God, Christ, Church: A Practical Guide to Process Theology*. New York: Crossroad, 1982.

Essay Two

Chronic shame starts when you're small and you don't feel safe with the people who are close to you. You need them to help you feel comfortable in yourself, but instead, when you're upset, hurt, or scared, there's nobody to comfort you, and you feel like you're falling apart all alone. That falling-apart feeling is shame. At the same time, shame is the one thing you can do about it: believe that the bad is in you, in what you need. That way, instead of falling apart, you have something that makes sense to you – your badness. After that, whenever things go wrong in your relationships and emotions, shame will have this story ready for you: it's because there's something wrong with you. But even though that story makes sense, it hurts, so shame also tells you to build a thick wall around this whole mess of needing and being wrong so that nobody knows about it – not even you, if you can help it.

How can shame be all these things? Isn't it one emotion like joy or sadness or fear? Yes, there is a specific emotion called shame, and I'll talk about that in a moment. What I'm describing here is how shame becomes a way of life, like having a chronic illness. The symptoms flare up every time you're feeling upset and there's nobody to help. Once that happens, the other things follow. It all gets put in motion whenever you feel misunderstood, disconnected, and alone with your feelings. And the more this sequence happens, the more time you will spend in that hurt and lonely place, believing you are the problem. This is the "illness" called chronic shame.

The specific emotion called shame is, by contrast, a one-time event of feeling bad, and it can happen to you at any age. It's what small children feel when they're old enough to know that a caregiver doesn't like what they're doing. Parents use it to teach their children about unacceptable behaviour, that it's not okay to hit people, for example. Hearing "That's not okay" changes something for a child. A comfortable

DOI: 10.4324/9781003499121-2

rhythm of relationship with their parent suddenly becomes uncomfortable. The back-and-forth easy regulation of emotion between the two of them is interrupted. This moment of dysregulated emotion could also be called a moment of shame.

Parents who work skillfully with momentary shame show their displeasure about behaviours without disconnecting from their children. They watch carefully for any calming or soothing their children might need, and they help them make the changes that will bring them back to feeling okay and connected again. Children may be coached to use their words instead of hitting or to say that they're sorry to someone whom they have hurt. They can be helped to accept a limit, or to think about their choices and their feelings.

In attentive caregiving, brief sequences of minor shame and active repair happen over and over. The focus is not on whether children are "good" or "bad" but rather on how they are learning to manage themselves in relationships. What happens if they're in conflict or make mistakes with other people? Lots of learning happens non-verbally, but when caregivers use words, they might say things like this:

> All your feelings are important. People can hurt your feelings and you can hurt other people's feelings. We can talk about your feelings and manage them together. We all make mistakes, and we can all say we're sorry and try to fix them. Usually, we can get what we need if we listen to each other and be fair. When things aren't fair, you can say so, and ask for change. Grownups are here to help you with these things.

This is an idealized, simplified picture, of course. I've pictured younger children; as children mature, helping them get through appropriate shame to accountability and self-respect becomes more complex. But I'm trying to make a simple point: There's a way to be with shame that moves toward wholeness. It doesn't deny harm done or culpability. In fact, it makes space in relationship to talk about emotions that are related to harm done – anger, fear, and sadness, along with shame. In this process, children learn that all parts of themselves are accepted, even parts that are learning to say sorry and to make different choices. As children grow, their relationships will become even more conflictual, their emotions more complicated, but they can also become more grounded in themselves as, with support from people who care for them, they keep working through brief, reparable experiences of shame.

Parents can hope that, with this grounding, their growing kids will be able to manage what their social worlds tell them about acceptable and unacceptable behaviour. If kids are shamed by systems that would make them either a "good kid" or a "bad kid," parents can help them get back to a sense of being a whole, good self who sometimes makes mistakes but who can also choose behaviours that are kind and fair.

Sadly, a social world may also sling destructive kinds of shame at kids. They may be shamed for their body size and shape, for their skin colour, for differences in their abilities to learn reading or math or sports, for their expressions of gender and sexuality, for their loudness or shyness, their clothes or shoes or hair. The list goes on, and such shaming lands; it hurts.

But children can learn that they can talk to somebody about what hurts. Parents can help them understand that shaming behaviour isn't acceptable, and that they don't have to participate in it or take it in. When children do get hurt by shame, they can know how to find the people who can be with them so that they can feel whole and good in themselves again.

What's it like to become an adult who has grown up feeling that there's somebody nearby who can feel your emotions with you and not be upset themselves or try to take over, that there's somebody to turn to when you feel bad about yourself? What's it like to have grown up with someone who can tell you, "It's not okay what you did, but I love you and I want to help you deal with it"? Likely you'll be an adult who can keep loving yourself as you deal with whatever you did that wasn't okay, an adult who can ask for help when shame strikes. If, growing up, you had help feeling whole again after shame events, you'll be far better equipped to face shame when it happens in your adult life, keep it to its right size, and reach out to others to repair what's broken and reconnect with them.

These healthy ways of working with shame have nothing in common with the process of chronic shame. Chronic shame leads to disintegration, not integration. In the chronic shame process, "wholeness" is something nobody can help you with. You have to try to create it for yourself – by always doing what you're supposed to do, for example, or by hiding out from human interaction that might trigger shame, or by staging performances of power or talent that mask what's going on inside. Inside, you don't feel solid, good, or whole. Your different feeling states don't balance out into a steady, comfortable identity. Your sense of self is shaky, and you spend a lot of energy trying to bolster it.

And you're doing all this alone. Your isolation leaves you vulnerable to any kind of shame the world throws at you about your body, mind, personality, or competence. If something bad seems to fit, you take it in like it's a deep truth about what's wrong with you. It may even be a strange relief to have something specific to blame for the bad feelings you have about yourself. But any specific kind of self-loathing is just one more symptom of chronic shame, an ongoing, pervasive state of fragmentation and dis-ease.

The process of chronic shame can begin even before we're old enough to feel the specific emotion of shame. That's because interpersonal disconnection can create dysregulated states in us almost from birth. Since 1978, Ed Tronick and colleagues have been using Still Face experiments to show how insistently infants as young as a month try to keep their caregivers engaged in "conversation," or a process we could call "mutual regulation." When the parent moves from normal engagement with their child to a non-engaged still face, the child does everything possible to regain the connection and then finally gives up, with body language that looks like a slump of despair or shame.[1]

In a 2010 video, where the little girl is a year old and very expressive about her expectations and her distress, it's a great relief to see the mom break out of one long minute of still face and bring her child back into happy connection.[2] As Tronick comments, the video clip shows us the good, the bad, and the ugly. The good is the remarkable social-emotional capacities infants have and use from birth. The bad is the distress that a non-response can cause – but we can also see the "bad" repaired very quickly. The ugly is to realize that for some infants the repair doesn't happen. They remain alone in the distress of disconnection.

Allan Schore has written volumes on how an infant's brain needs the interaction of a secure attachment relationship in order to develop properly.[3] He calls the crucial interaction "affect regulation" – a parent's consistent attuning to a baby's physiological and emotional states and responding in various ways, from the feeding, rocking, and crooning that soothe a baby's distress to the chatty interactions and small repetitive games that keep an alert baby engaged and content.

Attunement isn't intruding on or even hovering over the baby's space. It's just being nearby physically and emotionally, being present without anxiety, open to whatever the baby might communicate, and then responding to the baby's cues about how to meet a need. Many parents talk about the challenge of interpreting their baby's cries, the pleasure of discovering responses that help their baby get back to calm states, and the fun of creating animated, joyful states together.

Most parents don't know that their responses are shaping their baby's brain, the right hemisphere in particular. This is Schore's special interest: what should happen and what can go wrong in the development of a person's right-brain capacities, from infancy through adulthood. What should happen is connectedness between the lower parts of the right brain, where emotions (affects) are felt as physical states, and higher parts of the right brain that are able to communicate affects in relationships and to make felt patterns and meanings out of emotional and relational experience. A felt sense of coherent self, rooted in body and emotional memory (not in linear, logical thought – that's a left-brain job), is also a product of right-brain connectivity.

What can go wrong is what Tronick calls the ugly. The caregiver fails to attune to the baby's states, responding with emotional absence, or the caregiver responds to the baby in ways that intensify rather than soothe distress. In either case, the baby's bodily affect is not brought into the orbit of a calmer, more organized system of feeling and thinking; their system has to cope alone. But it can't, so after trying hard and protesting hard, the system shuts down, giving up on focus and coordination.

So driven by bodily feeling states and so dependent on others to regulate those states, infants and toddlers have whole-body responses to the distress of disconnection. When they give up trying to connect, a glaze of dissociation comes over them, a deflation or turning away, a blank stare. Later, when children have learned that trying hard to connect or protesting doesn't work, and when they have achieved some kind of self-regulation, their dissociation is less obvious. Children can learn to manage emotional disconnection by shutting down only their painful, falling-apart feelings; with their developing left-brain competence, they can carry on with other kinds of focus and coordination.

Nevertheless, the invisible effects of disconnection continue. As Schore says, attachment relationships shape the brain. The lack of right-brain connection between caregiver and child translates directly to gaps in connectivity in the child's right brain. When constantly threatened by overwhelming dysregulation, children dissociate emotional experience in general. Their visceral right-brain experience remains disconnected from higher-level right-brain processes that could hold this affective energy, calm it, sort it into patterns, and give words to it. Their most powerful emotions, never communicated in relationship, fail to become a conscious, rich, and vital aspect of their self-awareness.

A child's right-brain development becomes compromised when caregivers don't use their own right brains to calm and sort out emotion for their child until the child can begin to do it for themselves. If caregivers don't do this necessary right-brain regulation, it's most likely because they can't. Their own right brains are unavailable or have tenuous internal connectivity, and there would be reasons for that.

———————

My mother, for example, was so anxious that she would do the wrong thing with her colicky firstborn that she left me wailing as she read Dr. Spock to get instructions. The story goes that my father took the book from her, threw it across the trailer, put me belly down on his bare, warm chest, and I quieted. Soon after, my mother's mother came to visit, and she was able to calm me by holding me firmly under her breasts, their warmth against my belly. My mother told me that this didn't work for her. I don't think it was because there was something wrong with her breasts (though she thought there was; she believed I couldn't get enough milk from them, and I was soon put on formula, not unusual in 1953). What was wrong for my mother was her lack of confidence in her intuition, in the self her right brain held. She couldn't trust her body-self and emotional self just to be with me, and what I felt in her hands and body was her anxiety, not her right-brain presence.

I can only speculate, but I'd guess that my mother's self-experience reflected more of a repressive barrier between her right brain and her left brain than a dissociative barrier in her right brain. Her logical left brain, home of the good daughter and good wife who did things by the book (including the Bible), couldn't afford to know much about the messy stuff of instinct, desire, and emotion that lived on the other side. She always had some prurient interest in the other side, though, and the discomfort of her connection with the forbidden came through as sensitivity about germs and smells and in the disgust that came up for her around the many things that transgressed her sense of normal.

Schore calls this a split on the horizontal (right/left) plane of the brain, in contrast with the split that undermines up-and-down right-brain connectivity. In this split between right and left, both sides of the brain are fully developed, but a lot of the emotional information processed on the right side is repressed. The good news, if this is your issue, is that you were given enough consistent affect attunement to have a coherent right-brain sense of self; you can manage your emotions and relationships. The bad news is that big parts of your emotional/relational self come to feel wrong and have to be denied.[4]

Shame is palpable in this system as the great threat that keeps you from knowing about your forbidden feelings. This threat of feeling shame constrains your freedom, and unless you do something (like psychoanalytic psychotherapy) to make friends with that other side, this lurking shame will be a life-long companion, and in that sense chronic. But it's not the kind of chronic shame that is born of right-brain chaos and perpetuates a fragmented, incoherent sense of self, the kind of shame that lives inside as "there's something deeply, terribly wrong with me," the shame that was my father's lot in life, and one of the ways in which I have carried his likeness. (Though I also learned, with my mother's help, to keep my conscious awareness mostly on the left side of my brain.)

My dad controlled his inner chaos, his constant underlying emotional dysregulation, by doing things, all kinds of things, all the time. He could trust his ability to figure things out, to set a course and follow it through. His self-system was soothed by activities that promised the satisfaction of a job well done or a useful, beautiful product. One of the things he wanted to create was a family with many children; the reason my mother kept having babies, she once told me, was that having a new baby made him so happy. He was intuitively good with them – until there was something he couldn't control. Then his sense of powerlessness would wipe out his capacity to tune into a baby's or a young child's state. His inner chaos would erupt, and to control it, he would have to control the child's state, not attune to it. As the books say, a dysregulated adult can't help a dysregulated child.

When I was three months old, my parents brought me to Iowa for Christmas with family. We were staying in my father's parents' small house. My mother found her mother-in-law difficult, and my father had a complicated relationship with his mother's controlling need of him. With so much tension in the air, what happened with me was perhaps inevitable. I began to have screaming fits that ended with me holding my breath and passing out. My parents were understandably frightened, and they had no one to call (and no Internet) to tell them that this was not an unusual thing for a baby to do, and that as soon as the baby lost consciousness, she would start breathing on her own again, and be fine.

Instead, what happened was typical. When my screaming reached a certain pitch, my mother would be paralyzed with anxiety. My father would run with me to the bathroom and put me under a cold shower. Gasping at the shock, I would keep breathing. He might have been acting on his need to control my out-of-control behaviour, or he might have believed he was saving my life. Anyway, I've been told that after this happened a few times, I stopped holding my breath when I cried.

For my mother, this story reveals an early example of a problem with my temper, and it is also the first in a series on how I learned to be good. The next story happens when I'm nine months old, on the road with my parents to a church where my father was student preacher for the morning service. In the evening they returned but only to participate in worship. Since they had a baby, they sat in the back, and when I started to cry, my dad took me outside, spanked me, and told me not to cry. When he brought me back in, I didn't. This shows how early and how quickly I was able to learn.

Telling the story, my mother never seemed to notice misattunement to a baby's needs. She too wanted me to be good – her kind of good – if from a part of herself that was more regulated than my father was able to be. It seems the ends, a docile baby and an obedient child, could justify the means.

I do remember one time when she protested. We were in The Hague, I was six, my brother was two. I wonder if it happened during the time when my father was studying for his oral doctoral exam, which had been explained to me as a big event and a reason to be quiet in the apartment. In any case, it was after dinner, and my father was trying to impose his will on my brother, who was sitting in a high chair and crying. Maybe he hadn't eaten his food and he couldn't get down until he did, or maybe he was just supposed to stop crying. Or both. Anyway, he didn't stop, not even when my father yelled louder, and so my father sent me to bed in the room next door and then he turned off the lights – to frighten my brother into submission, I guess. My brother just wailed harder, and I heard my mother say just loudly enough to be heard, "Jim, he's scared!"

I don't remember what happened next. I hope that my father turned on the lights, and that my mother was allowed to lift her son from the high chair and comfort him. I remember what happened that night not because it was unusual for my father to impose his will on a child, but because it was unusual for my mother to speak. She risked his rage being turned on her, but she spoke. It was a surprise to me when she put words to what was happening, and that she said "scared." I didn't know my brother was scared, or that I was. I just didn't move, waiting for it to be over. Scared was what I felt when my father wasn't angry but he might be angry soon.

One time, that same year and in that same apartment in The Hague, my father made me very scared on purpose. I didn't know why I was in trouble with my father, and my mother wasn't saying. I must have told her that the boys I played with in the alley had been mean to me. Maybe they wouldn't let me ride their bikes, which I always wanted to do. But anyway, my mother somehow thought they had been interfering with me in some sexual way. That's the sense I've been able to make of it since. She must have said that to my dad, and so we were sitting together in the living room, my dad across a coffee table from me. "What did those boys do to you?" he asked sternly. I didn't even know what boys he meant, but I said they hadn't done anything to me. He pulled his belt out from his belt loops, folded it in his hand, and told me, "If you ever let those boys do anything to you, I will do this to you," and he brought the belt down with a loud crack on the table. "Do you understand?" I didn't, and I could hardly breathe or move, but I nodded yes. My mom didn't say anything.

———————

These are hard stories for me to tell, and maybe they are hard to read, too. Perhaps, I should remind you (and me) that my dad and mom loved their children and were deeply committed to being responsible parents. Maybe I should say that this same year when I turned six, I was given the Child's Story Bible for my birthday and I liked hearing it read aloud after dinner, and on Sundays, we went for walks to the park and fed bread to the ducks, and on Sinterklaas Day, there was a paint-by-numbers set and a big chocolate letter "P" for me and a "J" for my little brother, and a funny hand-puppet, too. But that would be circling around the point, which is not to decide, "How bad was it?" The point is: a chronic shame process starts because something *happens*. The point is: these are the kinds of things that happen, if differently across generations and subcultures, and the essence of what happens is that children who have suffered an assault to their nervous system are left alone with their need and desire to be held until they feel whole again. No one holds them. And then their fragmented needy and desiring self becomes, to them, what's wrong.

Conscious, wilful child abuse is also something that happens, with an aftermath of survivors' chronic shame. Those stories are far more difficult to tell and to hear. But I don't think I need to tell you that kind of story to help you understand theory about chronic shame. The theory speaks of a child's overwhelming distressing affect and inability to manage it, about caregivers' repetitive failures to attune to and regulate that affect, and about the dissociation and fragmentation that follow within that child's right-brain experience of self and self-with-other. I think the stories I have told illustrate the basics of that theory.

I have many reasons to be glad my experience wasn't horrific; one of them is that I can tell clients that they don't need to be ashamed of feeling bad about themselves when they can't identify terrible trauma in their childhood. I can say that although terrible trauma didn't happen to them, I believe that nevertheless something did happen, something powerful and important, and we can get a feel for it together. We listen to the stories they remember, and inevitably a picture emerges of a profound mismatch between the emotional connection they needed as children and what was available to them.

I may not use this theoretical language, but it's usually clear to me that none of the adults in the picture had enough access to a mature enough, integrated enough right brain to do the critical work of attuning to and regulating a child's affect. If my clients say, "But I had such big intense feelings," I tell them that kids are supposed to have big intense feelings. And then of course the feelings get bigger and more intense if they're not understood. If clients assure me that their parents didn't intend to hurt them, I agree.

I did not intend to hurt my firstborn when she was eighteen months and suddenly ran into the street. I ran out and grabbed her; maybe a car was coming, or maybe not, but in any case, I was scared. I gave her three whacks on her diapered bottom and said loudly, "NO! DON'T GO IN THE STREET!" What was I thinking? I wasn't thinking. What did that teach her? To be scared of me, in my angry-scared state. What was I doing? I was parenting as I had been parented. Thank God I had some help learning how to parent differently even while I was still working toward emotional coherence. My parents, like so many parents, didn't have help.

This essay is about shame and falling apart. You can see how it happens – to me or my brother or the child in your mind as you follow along with the theory. There's overwhelming affect, there's no one to regulate it, and then there's disintegration. What does it feel like to disintegrate? I can't say, and maybe nobody can. Human systems quickly dissociate affect that's too much to bear. Think of the adult experience of sudden humiliation: you freeze; you can't think or feel; you just want to disappear, feel nothing, be nothing. Dissociation is purposeful and protective. When disorganized affect floods your right brain, you lose access to it. Then, if you're lucky, other parts of your brain step in to take over.

My left brain stepped in quickly and easily when I was a child. My mother helped out with books that would explain things to me and teach me to be good – the Grabby Pup book, for example.[5] He was a bad puppy because he grabbed all the other animals' toys. So one night his mother dog collected all the toys and put them in the middle of the room. Grabby Pup had to walk round and round them all night long and not take a single toy – and he didn't. After that night, he never again took any of the other animals' toys. Hooray! He wasn't Grabby any more! The last page of the book asked, "So what name would you give to a puppy with long silky hair and soft floppy ears?" To me, Grabby was his name, and I could never think of a different one. I knew that the story was also telling me not to be grabby. I don't know whether I made that connection for myself or my mother helped me with it.

By the time I was eight, I was the big kid with three little siblings, and responsibility became my identity. My mom didn't have time to teach me much except how to pin diapers on the clothesline, run the washing machine, and iron my dad's shirts. I was quite good at ironing, and she paid me a quarter when I had finished a basketful. She told me I had to learn not to be greedy about food – this was after I had helped myself to seconds when there were guests at the table – and she played board games with me on Saturday nights so that I could get better about losing. (This would be after she put rollers in my freshly washed hair so that it could be curly on Sunday morning.) But mostly my learning was turned over to school.

In Omaha, my parents sent me to a Lutheran parochial school a long bus ride from home. I didn't have friends in my neighbourhood, but the school became a home for me, a place where I was never in trouble and adults were kind. The school was kindergarten through eighth grade in three rooms, three grades to a room, with only five to ten kids in a grade, the same kids year after year. I was free to do my work fast and then do whatever I wanted, quietly. I could listen in on the other classes or get a book from the classroom library. When I had read all the books in the younger grades' library, I was allowed to go downstairs and get books from the older grades' library.

The best part of school was recess because I could play sports with the boys. In the winter, I could stuff my skirt into my snowpants and shoot baskets. In the fall, we played flag football, and as soon as the snow melted, it was baseball. The school principal, who also taught the oldest kids, let me play on the boys' teams in our small Lutheran school league, even though I had to wear dresses to school and to games. I never got to quarterback even though I could throw a long pass. Nobody would let a girl quarterback; I knew that. I knew I was lucky to play.

Every year our principal taught us to act and sing for an all-school musical. He would play the piano. On Friday afternoons he taught us art, like how to draw things with perspective and shading. Once I heard my mother say to someone that he might be a little effeminate, you know. She had that look on her face, but I didn't care. He was my teacher; she didn't know anything about him.

The principal's daughter, who had graduated from the school a year before I got to his class, was tall and beautiful, and one day she came back to give us a concert on her marimba. Her hands moved so fast you could hardly see them, and her music filled the classroom. When she finished, the room was very quiet, and she smiled at her father who was standing at the wall nearby. He smiled back, and I saw that they had felt the music together. I saw that she was special to him.

Halfway through eighth grade, my first year in Mississippi, I found the Omaha school address on a report card I had kept, and I wrote my teacher/principal a letter to say two things: (one) how great it was to be in a school with so many kids and find out that I was smart, and (two) how great it was to be able to play on a real girls' basketball team. He wrote back to tell me he was glad to hear I was happy in my new school.

I was stumbling into adolescence with my identity of helpful daughter and responsible big sister. I needed more, and then these other kinds of specialness just fell on me and saw me through high school. I didn't hang out with friends, but I was good to have on teams and the student council. I didn't go to dances or proms because there were no boys who looked at me and I didn't look at them, not like that. Girls couldn't wear pants to school, so I wore kilt-style skirts, button-up shirts and no-sock loafers. Sometimes I would try a real dress; I could do it for church on Sunday, even add make-up and heels, but I just felt stupid in a dress at school. School was where I could be smart and do sports, end of story. I thought people saw my strangeness, but I also thought they saw me being good at stuff and therefore happy. I played along at being happy, and when I won academic awards and was a star basketball player, I guessed I was as happy as I was going to be.

Basketball mattered most. I still have a scrapbook of clippings from the town newspaper, tiny paragraphs at first. I underlined my name and points scored before I pasted them in. The point totals got larger, and the stories longer. The last page of the scrapbook is a full-page story and a photo of me (awkward in a dress I hated) with the caption, "Miss DeYoung is Miss Everything." It was written when I had recently played in the State All-Star game and had been awarded an all-expenses academic scholarship to college. My grown kids have teased me about Miss Everything, but with gentleness toward a mom who once needed to underline and paste in evidence that she mattered.

Basketball was also the only place where I could be greedy to win and play ferociously and it was all good. If I played a clean game, even blocking out hard with my hips and clearing a lane with elbows flying, there was no way I could be too much. On the basketball court, I was myself in my muscles and skin, in my shiny uniform and my Converse All-Stars. For the purposes of this essay, I'd say that the physical intensity and controlled aggression of playing basketball was the only way, in those days, that my non-verbal emotional energy made it out into the world.

For the purposes of this essay, I should also talk about falling apart after the awards banquet my junior year. It was for both the boys' and girls' teams and their coaches. First we ate our steak dinner and then the awards were given out, small trophies for best offensive, best defensive, most improved, and so forth, the large MVP trophy saved until last. The awards had been decided by a team vote, secret ballot, with coaches getting to vote, too. I had our team's scoring record; sportswriters had put me (and nobody else) on the all-conference team. But I was awarded no trophies that night. When the MVP went to somebody else, my coach caught my eye with a look that said "Watch yourself, Pat. Be a good loser." It was still not my strength.

I went very still and numb as I waited for the event to be over. I don't remember leaving the cafeteria or getting to the car. I do remember stopping the car on a country road in the dusk, knowing that I couldn't drive home yet. When I finally sat still, the pain I felt was shocking, more intense than physical injury. I felt the humiliation of losing (did my teammates not like me, or even hate me? I had no idea) and also deep shame that it all mattered so much more to me than it should have. I felt the shame of being so very vulnerable, of needing to get a trophy, even as I felt how shattered I was not to get one. I didn't cry. I just waited for the pain to ease and my functioning self to come back.

After a while I was able to drive home. It was a Friday night. By Monday when I went to school, I could act normal.

The next year was different, but as I write about this now, it's clear to me that those accolades barely touched me compared to what shame had done to me the year before. Adding to my scrapbook was never a celebration; it was tending to my talisman against falling apart. The things I pasted into the book walled out my feelings of being empty and alien.

My system for trying to feel okay was fragile, but I didn't have another way to do life. I was just then leaving home to try to find my way into adulthood. Big things were expected of me. This was no time to fall apart, so I didn't. Here's what I did instead.

I lasted three semesters of my four-year free ride at the college in Mississippi. I lived in the dorm and played varsity basketball; I curled my hair and put on hose and heels to go to class; I aced exams. But I was also thinking about the meaning of life, my life; I was nineteen. I knew that becoming a powerhouse Southern belle wasn't going to do it for me. (This college had once produced a Miss America. The messaging wasn't subtle.)

I didn't know how badly I wanted something else until the boys came to visit, six of them sitting around our table, packing away my mom's lasagna. They had come from their CRC college in Iowa to investigate my dad's seminary; the CRC seminary in Michigan was getting liberal, they thought, and so these pre-sem guys were checking out a more conservative option. I remember one funny, nerdy guy, a jock and a skinny scholar who were best friends, and the tallest boy, with curly black hair and bright blue eyes. My parents lit up in the presence of these boys from home. I felt strangely excited, and I hoped it was because of the boys since I hadn't ever felt anything for a boy. Maybe I just had to find the right boys, and they weren't in Mississippi.

It suddenly occurred to me that my parents might let me take a semester away at the boys' college. I knew exactly where Dordt College was: on the edge of the small town of Sioux Center, Iowa. It was named after the Canons of Dort, one of the three Confessions of Faith of the CRC, and also after the town, Dordrecht, Netherlands, where these canons were drawn up in 1618–1619 as a polemic against a movement seeking to soften the doctrine of predestination. Dordt's magazine of student essays, poems, and short stories was called *The Canon*. The school colours were black and white. It had begun as a two-year teachers' college when CRC farming communities in north-west Iowa needed staff for their bourgeoning Christian schools. By 1973, it was a small, four-year liberal arts college, and its professors had roots in Dutch Reformed communities across the US, Canada, and the Netherlands.

None of these details mattered to me. I was just drawn to a feeling of home. If the American deep South wasn't home, where could I belong in the world? When we'd lived in Omaha, our family had visited Sioux Center often. The biggest CRC church in town had called my father to his Omaha home missionary position, and so he reported to them from the field. College students who helped him in the summer came from Dordt. Sometimes we visited Sioux Center to catch up with people who had been my parents' friends in college or seminary. The tenor who had once set up their blind date became a Dordt English professor, happily married to someone who wasn't my aunt the pianist. My parents called these friends "Cope and Sal," and I had liked how the grownups laughed together every time we visited.

And then there were the fields of corn and soybeans, the big sky, the sense of Midwest farm in my blood, the aunts and uncles living nearby. I had no words for my strange homesickness. All I needed to tell my parents was that I would like to spend a semester at Dordt. Once I could assure my dad that the Mississippi scholarship wouldn't be affected by a semester away, they were completely behind the idea. Maybe my parents liked the look of those boys for me, too.

Eight weeks later I started classes, one of them with "Cope," and I relished his delighted double-take when he recognized me and introduced me to the class as the daughter of his old best friend. As I settled into my philosophy, literature, and history courses, as I went to breakfast and dinner, chapel, church, and coffee with CRC kids all bearing Dutch last names, I realized that it wasn't the boys that drew me; it was the chance of belonging, and in that belonging to find the meaning of life. Seriously. And to be honest, it was also a great liberation to go to class in jeans and a sweatshirt.

I talked my parents into another semester. Then, during that semester, I wrote a letter home to say I wanted to stay to graduate because here I could feel the meaning of my faith, a rare bit of self-disclosure. I asked my father to talk to the Dean in Mississippi and apologize on my behalf. I felt like I was walking out on a deal, but I also thought it wouldn't matter much to anyone. My father acted on his sense of parental and pastoral responsibility, I guess, but he told me later that it wasn't fun.

I didn't see much of the pre-sem boys in school since they had to take things like Greek, Hebrew, and Church History. Once the skinny scholar asked for a date and I had to say no, though I felt bad for hurting his feelings. I admired the tall boy with bright blue eyes from a distance. He had a girlfriend. I think I knew that I didn't want to be with him; I wanted to BE him: handsome and confident in his knowledge that he was going to be somebody who mattered, doing something important. I couldn't change my gender and go to seminary. But now I had a bigger, better option; I was studying Christian philosophy.

The kind of Christian philosophy I learned was complicated. It teaches that there's a grid you can lay on the entire history of Western philosophies so that as you read them you can see embedded in each system one of a series of dichotomies, all false from a Christian perspective. There's a structure of reality rooted in the principles of creation, and once you understand those principles, you can find God's truth to bring to all sorts of human endeavours and conundrums. Most importantly, there's a world-and-life view, a belief system, undergirding what anyone writes or says or does in the world, and you can figure out what that is. In that sense, for everyone, all of life is religion. Everyone may not know this, but we do. And all of this matters far beyond the academy; it has implications for politics, law, ethics, education, aesthetics, and more. Furthermore, it will show us how we can bring peace and justice into the world through what we do in our everyday lives.

This was the meaning of life I found in the cornfields of Iowa, transplanted in the late 1960s from the lecture halls of the Free University of Amsterdam. There have been worse principles to stake a young life on. I was practical enough to know that I wouldn't make my living as a Christian philosopher, so I majored in English as well as in philosophy, and I got a secondary teaching certificate so that I could get a job when I graduated.

In my search for my life's purpose and meaning, I was now doing my parents' life – only better, as I saw it. Where they had been wrong in their philosophy and politics, I would be right. There was the glitch about gender; I could not be a leader in the church. But that was just as well, because the institution of church would stifle this new energy. I would work around the glitch to make my own contribution.

Apples do not fall far from trees. This new version of doing good in the world had the same old flaw embedded in it. The theory overlooked human tragedy and desolation; it didn't attend to relational risk, rupture, and negotiation; it didn't have language for working through emotional pain. In terms I use as shorthand, the system looked away from the emotional/relational realities of the human right brain. As an essentially left-brain system of making meaning, it would leave a trail of emotional incoherence and shame in its wake.

I said in my first essay that I don't believe that emotional repression is inherent in religion itself. Here I will add that many systems of making meaning in life have nothing to do with religion but still fail in their own way to attend to the relational and emotional vulnerabilities of being human. This can happen in all kinds of subcultures where certain things matter most – making money, expanding science and technology, upholding justice, producing art – or you can add your own example. Religion is just the example I know.

Fast forward, in my example of making sense of life, to a full decade after I had graduated from high school as Miss Everything, and some years after finding meaning and purpose at the college in Iowa.

I was living in Toronto, having married a boy named Nigel who had studied Christian philosophy with me. We had been friends first, and then I had noticed, experimentally, that when we kissed, I could feel arousal and desire. That was a good surprise. But what sealed the deal was our shared vision for a meaningful life. We married after our last year at Dordt, and it didn't take long for us to move to Toronto, the

North American home base of our Christian philosophy. We came to find a community of people who promoted the vision we wanted to carry forward. He was Canadian and I was happy to immigrate.

We now had two children and were expecting a third. I had never taught high school English, but I had used up my four-year graduate scholarship and was doing TA work for the University of Toronto English Department, teaching forestry students the grammar of sentences. I had nothing left to do but finish the dissertation, but I had lost heart. I was doing the graduate program only because near the end of my undergrad, Dordt College had nominated me to compete for a graduate award, and then I won it. A PhD seemed the next thing I was supposed to do. I tried to imagine my degree as being useful somehow to what we called kingdom work, but I couldn't see it. I wanted to finish what I had started – all that time, money, energy, and to come so far, be so close. But I didn't care about the project.

I cared about my family, and about the alternative community we had settled into, like a tiny town within the big city. Some of us had started a scattered unit housing co-op, and many of us lived in it. We ran a food co-op; we shared maternity clothes and childcare, pot-luck dinners and camping trips, tools, and rented vehicles. People bent their emerging careers toward making differences for good.

For many of us, the centre of this life together was a church. It had begun as a CRC university campus ministry, but as life took people away from the university and into jobs, families, and a housing co-op on the other side of town, we set ourselves up as a congregation that met in an east end Anglican church basement. We would be clergy-free; we would do it ourselves. This caused some kerfuffle in CRC governing bodies, but in the end, we were allowed to carry on with minimal oversight.

Most of us had grown up in church, and we took our tasks seriously. Committees met regularly. Nigel worked on liturgy. I was on preaching/teaching: five or six of us would meet to work out our next group of texts and themes and then we'd each take a Sunday. At first, I was nervous, but it turned out I had a gift for preaching. The gift took some work: Early in my week, I would go to a theological college on the U of T campus and read through commentaries on the text and its context. Then I would think about my listeners. An alternative religious community attracts wounded souls – nobody comes to a basement just to do church on a Sunday; everybody is seeking meaning for their particular fraught and complex life. This vulnerability would be there, just under the surface. In my prep, I would wonder how my text could connect with such human need, and I would leave the question lie for a day or two.

Then it would come to me and I would start to write my script. Once I knew where I was going, I would know how to tell the God-story embedded in the text and context. This God was never angry; this God was reaching out to guide, strengthen, and comfort. I would use my words and voice to bring the version of God revealed in the text right up next to what I knew of the vulnerability in the room. I understand now that I was first of all preaching to myself, asking my own right brain to find my own inarticulate pain. Which is not to say that my sermons were bogus. Perhaps this gave them what truth and power they had.

I was almost twenty-eight, my little girls were four and one, I was pregnant, it was fall and time for me to register for another year of trying to write a dissertation that didn't matter. I wanted out. I floated the idea with Nigel. It wasn't like I'd be quitting a job; the only money I made now came from piecework copy editing I was doing on the side, and there was plenty in the pipeline. He said it was up to me and he meant it. So I decided. I notified the graduate department that I was withdrawing from the program, and I packed all my notes and drafts into a cardboard box and took it to the curb. The next day it was gone. I expected to feel relief, but I felt nothing.

Not long after, Nigel decided he would quit his graduate program too and train to become an elementary school teacher. I didn't have a plan. I didn't know that my self-system had a plan: it was time for me to begin to fall apart.

Such falling apart can be the best thing that happens to you if you're locked into defences against chronic shame, but at the time, it feels like the worst.

―――――――

The strange truth is, the falling apart has already happened – a long time ago when you couldn't bear to feel it. Behind a barrier of dissociation, your feelings are already lying tangled and pulsing with broken energy. What needs to fall apart is the way you've put your life and self together so as not to feel them. This won't mean coming up with the True Story of your life. It will mean opening up to your right-brain feelings in all their messy chaos and slowly making emotional sense of them. The first disintegration happened because there was nobody there to help; your system can make its move now because it senses that somebody could be there this time. In the self you've constructed, however, that's the last thing you want – to have to tell somebody you're falling apart, that you need help. Opportunity will have to arrive as crisis.

I was, indeed, no longer so alone. Nigel was no more adept at emotional/relational process than I was, but he was a steady presence of acceptance and love. Community presence was everywhere. We shared life, even if I didn't share my feelings. I've told you about my preaching. Also, every Sunday morning someone invited prayer requests from the group before community prayer time. People mentioned issues in the city or the world, projects or causes that needed our prayers. But they also spoke about sick kids, parents dying back home, difficult decisions to make. I don't remember anyone ever saying, "I'm having a terrible time emotionally; these are dark days for me; I'm worried about my mental health." I do remember that when someone was having a hard time recovering from a birth, we prayed for her health. Only later did I realize it had been postpartum depression.

We were idealists, intellectuals, activists. We were also moving out of our twenties, out of grad school to whatever work we could find. We had to pay bills, make our relationships work, take care of our kids with and without daycare. Sometimes the messes in our kitchens and our marriages loomed larger than the messes in the world. The church community began to meet in "household groups" on Sunday evenings – six or eight people who came together in group members' homes to talk more intimately about how we felt in our daily lives, what we struggled with, the kind of meanings we still tried to make of it all.

In this group, in my own home, I broke my silence. That night there were only four of us there, and we had known the other couple since Dordt days. I was feeling bad, I said. They responded kindly, with gentle questions. I remember searching for words and sentences, fighting off shame, but I don't remember the conversation, only how it ended.

I agreed I needed help, and that I would find a therapist. Nigel was witness and he helped me follow through, though this conclusion had shocked both of us.

The therapist, too, was kind and her questions were gentle. She saw that the end of the PhD meant I had lost my identity as smart and special. She helped me see that being a mom plus being pregnant was stressful. She gave me a vocational preference test to help me start to look ahead. I saw her just once every two weeks, all we could afford even with a sliding scale. Maybe that's how she came to give me the homework assignment. It was clear: Write me a page about your relationship with your mother, and another page about your relationship with your father.

I wrote simple, true things I had never thought about before. Then I began to feel things I had never felt before. But I didn't know how to talk about them, dark heavy feelings like huge stones in my chest, like I would never feel okay again. It was late November, then December. I didn't want to go out of the house or have anyone in. Feeling guilty and ashamed, I cancelled my trip to my sister Lou's wedding. I took care of my kids and struggled to concentrate on editing copy. A few days before Christmas, the weight of darkness was crushing. I called the therapist for help, but she was away. I found a therapist who could see me. I didn't know how to say what was wrong, but I brought him some poems I had tried to write. He read them and then he asked me, "What's the one thing these are all about, Pat?" I looked at him, clueless. "Pain," he said. "You are in pain."

I saw him once a week until my son was born in March, and then resumed for a few months after. When I ended with him, I could parse "pain" – identify the anger, disappointment, and sadness I felt in relationship with my parents. I could see how my family system worked. I had dared to have hard conversations with Nigel, though we both always wanted to avoid conflict. I had read books on counselling and found that I wanted to be a therapist. To guarantee employment, I would get a social work degree, but to get into the program, I needed prerequisites. I started those one evening course at a time. I went back into my community, back to church, and eventually started preaching again.

It looked like I had done my falling apart and was now reassembled, having integrated an emotional self who had been a stranger to me.

That was somewhat true. But other things were also true. I had only begun to make contact with my troubled, fragmented emotional self. And my reassembly was done on the only pattern I knew: to use my mind to make sense, to make things happen, to re-invent myself on a more sustainable model.

My competence came back to me, but the pain didn't leave. It hung on as low-level anxious depression that persisted underneath everything, including my plans for the future. But in this future, therapy was positive, a discipline and a practice that could help people feel better. I was going to learn that discipline and practice! And so, on my way toward a social work degree, I went back to therapy with reasons to hope. I hoped to feel better, cured. I might have imagined a grace that would put me all back together again, a kind of Humpty Dumpty miracle.

But now I'm thinking about how grace moves within processes of falling apart. There's no grace in a child's disintegration when there's nobody there to hold and comfort. But there's grace in dissociation itself, protection against feeling what's too much to bear. There's also grace in the mind's capacity to remember unconsciously and to wait for a time to reconnect and integrate.

Ironically, it was the imposition of so-called grace that governed my time of waiting and the self I could construct. Home and church gave me security enough to become functional and responsible in the world. My apparent success was also due to privilege: I was born with a strong body and vigorous mind to parents who were white, educated professionals living in the relative affluence and safety of mid-century, midwestern America. But that's not the kind of grace I mean; it's just the luck of the birth lottery.

I'm ashamed now that I bought into the self-righteousness of my tradition, its assumption that it holds God's own definition of truth, and its illusion that this definition is good news for all the world. But I also know first-hand how convincing an illusion of specialness can be when you live within it. In our Toronto community, I may have needed the illusion more than most and therefore needed to crash out harder. I know that many of my peers used the questioning spirit of our church community to find their way to faith that would sustain humble, respectful engagement with other good people in the world no matter what their cultural or religious tradition. I don't imagine that these peers felt such transformation as a falling apart.

In its second decade, our church itself began to fall apart, and its members decided to end it formally, to acknowledge both gratitude and grief. At the goodbye service, as we sat in a big circle for the last time, two things were clear to me. First, this group had provided a safe sense of home for me through a long vulnerable time in my life. Second, members were now spending their life energies on all sorts of things besides church; in real-life terms, the project was no longer sustainable. As it came to its own natural end, this strange, small church released people to carry elsewhere whatever they had struggled for in that place.

As necessary endings go, this one was not terribly painful. I'm thinking, by contrast, of stories clients have told me of running from reality until they're at the very edge of a sustainable life. Something has to give, or end. They come saying, "I can't do this anymore," and "this" can be anything from chasing success with ninety-hour work weeks, to taking care of every suffering person in their orbit, to compulsive escapes into hook-up sex or substance use. They are harsh with themselves and full of despair about their choices.

I don't tell them that their obsession with success or self-sacrifice or partying has been a good thing. I agree that their MO has done them harm, but I also say this, as many times over as the harshness emerges: *Your way of doing life has been the best you could do to feel okay and keep going. We need to be kind to the "you" who has been suffering far more than you know and trying so hard not to feel it.*

Whatever kept them from feeling their shamed vulnerability worked until it didn't. An inner balance has shifted, and now they'll have to find a different way to feel okay. It's a sad truth that people in chronic emotional pain can switch up their obsessions and addictions interminably, exchanging one MO for another that promises a new kind of escape. But if these troubled people turn up in my office, I can guess that they're falling apart now not just because their escapes have turned into traps but also because there's a modicum of emotional safety in their lives. Human connection has touched them somehow, and that's why they have come to a therapist to talk, even though "just talking" makes no sense and promises no fix.

The meaning of life I grabbed onto at nineteen protected me from feeling, but it also allowed me to belong to a group that felt passion for a cause. This was far better than being a lonely alien. Years of living in such a community reassured me unconsciously that if I fell apart, I would not be alone.

I'm saying that grace isn't what appears after the times of falling apart; it runs right through those times. Grace is where the power of love in the universe makes contact with the pain of being human. Grace is in our drive to escape pain and make sense of life, whether righteously or misguidedly or even self-destructively. Grace is the particles and waves of energy that interrupt destruction and lure us toward hope and wholeness; thus, there's grace in the pain of hitting the end of the line and in coming to understand that self-deception may also have been self-protection, which can open to something new. Grace is present wherever human connection gets through to lonely aliens who don't even know what they are missing. It's the inkling that there might be more connection and wholeness for you if you can let yourself fall in that general direction. Grace is in the falling.

NOTES

1 Edward Tronick, Heidelise Als, Lauren Adamson, Susan Wise, and T. Berry Brazelton, "The Infant's Response to Entrapment between Contradictory Messages in Face-to-Face Interaction," *Journal of Child Psychiatry* 17 (1978): 1–13.

2 Edward Tronick, "The 'Still Face' Experiment," UMass Boston, March 12, 2010, YouTube video, 8:33, https://youtu.be/VmE3NfB_HhE

3 Allan Schore, *Affect Regulation and the Origin of the Self* (Mahwah, NJ: Erlbaum, 1994); *Affect Dysregulation and Disorders of the Self* (New York: Norton, 2003); *Affect Regulation and the Repair of the Self* (New York: Norton, 2003); *The Science of the Art of Psychotherapy* (New York: Norton, 2012).

4 Allan Schore, *The Development of the Unconscious Mind* (New York: Norton, 2019); *Right Brain Psychotherapy* (New York: Norton, 2019).

5 Nancy Raymond, *Grabby Pup* (Grand Rapids, MI: Fideler, 1945).

REFERENCES

Schore, Allan. *Affect Regulation and the Origin of the Self.* Mahwah, NJ: Erlbaum, 1994.

Schore, Allan. *Affect Dysregulation and Disorders of the Self.* New York: Norton, 2003.

Schore, Allan. *Affect Regulation and the Repair of the Self.* New York: Norton, 2003.

Schore, Allan. *The Science of the Art of Psychotherapy*. New York: Norton, 2012.

Schore, Allan. *The Development of the Unconscious Mind*. New York: Norton, 2019.

Schore, Allan. *Right Brain Psychotherapy*. New York: Norton, 2019.

Raymond, Nancy. *Grabby Pup*. Grand Rapids, MI: Fideler, 1945.

Tronick, Edward. "The 'Still Face' Experiment." UMass Boston, March 12, 2010. YouTube video, 8:33, https://youtu.be/VmE3NfB_HhE.

Tronick, Edward, Heidelise Als, Lauren Adamson, Susan Wise, and T. Berry Brazelton. "The Infant's Response to Entrapment between Contradictory Messages in Face-to-Face Interaction." *Journal of Child Psychiatry* 17 (1978): 1–13.

Essay Three

The animal species *homo sapiens* exists in families, clans, and tribes. We carry our sociability in our nervous systems, in the very same body–brain wiring that alerts us to danger and activates responses such as fight, flight, and freeze. When threat recedes, the energy of our nervous systems can come back from defensive states into a calm, receptive state that allows for social engagement. Stephen Porges calls this a ventral vagal state, named after the part of the vagus nerve that runs through the front of our bodies, including the parts of our feeling-selves we know as faces, hearts, and bellies. It's activated by and supports safe social engagement.[1]

To thrive as humans, we need to be sociable, and we can't be sociable unless we feel safe. Learning how to rest, interact, and explore while feeling safely connected with others may be more complicated for some of us than others. We might be differently abled in our vision, hearing, or neural processing of information; we might have been born highly sensitive and prone to anxious states of over-stimulation. If, however, our nearby, caring people feel mostly safe themselves, they will find the specific ways of responding to us that help us learn to be calm and present with them. The basics are quite simple. To feel safe, humans need other humans to approach them with a posture that's open and non-threatening, with eyes and faces that communicate friendly, non-intrusive interest. Certain kinds of smiling help. Porges emphasizes voice quality: a calm way of speaking that varies in intonation, but not in loudness/softness.

Our social engagement systems will stay available to us if our nervous systems don't constantly need to fight or hide or go numb to protect us from human danger. The front of our bodies, from face to belly, can be open, soft, and warm toward people who can be open, soft, and warm toward us – except for the times when we actually

DOI: 10.4324/9781003499121-3

need protection, and then our systems can step in fast and well to shield our vulnerability. This is one way to describe basic psychological and emotional health.

It's so easy to think of psychological trouble as a disembodied, mysterious personal affliction that sometimes becomes powerful enough to affect our physical systems and our relationships. Psychotherapy helps us demystify a "troubled mind" by helping us understand that our psychological trouble has a lot to do with our early relationships, trouble that we've carried forward into our present relationships with ourselves and with others. It also helps us realize that emerging from our trouble will require some changes in present relationships.

Then we come back around to our "troubled mind" in a completely different way. Change in how we can be with ourselves and others is hard, slow work because past and present relationship trouble keeps directly affecting our brain and nervous system. Because our attachment people lacked the right-brain calm and coherence to help us learn to manage emotion, there are things we haven't learned to do. This was the story behind the last essay: the right-brain experience of falling apart, being alone with overwhelming, unprocessed feeling, and then finding safety in dissociation, protection behind a wall of shame. If our young emotional self is dissociated, walled off, we can't learn how to be emotionally connected with others.

In adulthood, if our right brains are not very available to us or if we can connect only to incoherent feelings, we won't be very comfortable in the emotional parts of relationships. We'll have a hard time bringing our emotional self forward, not trusting that anyone would want to be with who we are inside. We can't really "do" the emotions of relationship, especially not the intense or difficult ones. Yet relationship is supposed to be one of the deep, abiding pleasures of being a person.

Polyvagal theory is another way to talk about how we end up missing something deep and important in our experience of self-with-others, a missing that turns into chronic shame. Like right-brain theory, polyvagal theory confirms that chronic shame isn't something essentially wrong with our mind. Our trouble is that since we were little, we haven't been able to trust the important people in our lives to be open to us with warmth and softness. Even subtle violation or neglect, when these experiences are constant, can wipe out our chances of living in a safe ventral vagal ambience of belonging. Ever after, just the presence of people may be enough to set off an anxious alert in our nervous system. A system rarely on red alert can still be almost always on orange, and with fight/flight systems at the ready, there's no uncomplicated space to learn social engagement by doing it. Yet this is exactly what would help us feel more comfortable and at home with other humans.[2]

———————

It might be better not to know about this state of affairs, about needing things that we can't even reach for. As I consider how I'm implicated in all of it, I slip and fall into shame about my own shame. Knowing that this is a common fall for shamed people doesn't make me feel any better sitting down here in the mud at the bottom of the hill. I hear my eleven-year-old self say, *Putting your thoughts into writing says that they matter*, and I know how much I have used writing to communicate with imaginary people who are happy to listen to me and understand me fully.

What makes me cringe, muttering here in the cold mud, is how transparent my strategy is. Anyone can see that I'm writing to make myself feel better, to have the illusion of connection in spite of what I don't know and can't do. The problem is that anyone can *see*. The problem is my relational shame as I anticipate how I will be received. In this instance, I imagine subtle scorn, ridicule, and disgust.

Right here and now, I have replicated the way chronic shame makes relationships hard for me. Here, my imagined "other" is not very safe at all, not open to feelings, hardly warm and soft! My self holds up badly against scorn and disgust, real or imagined. My right brain shuts down. I protect my face, heart, and belly. What do I need to say to myself so that I can keep writing and stay out of the puddle of mud at the bottom of the hill? Three things.

First, I do know that writing isn't a reciprocal or mutual activity. I do all the talking and wanting to be understood. In fairness to myself, though, that doesn't mean I'm shamefully self-centred; when I read what others write, I'm responding to their quests for understanding. Writing and reading are slow, careful kinds of sharing that are legitimate in their own terms. There's no shame in wanting to write well or in imagining readers who could be delighted or moved by what I write.

Second, I do know that writing is one thing and face-to-face emotional connection with real people in my life is another. Writing will never help me to see them clearly, and it won't even make me matter more to them. People who love me will love me no less if I do a bad piece of writing. At this time in my life, I don't do writing instead of talking. I can access interpersonal courage as well as the courage to write.

Third, these essays ask of me the writerly courage to find what needs to be said in a voice that is my own. Dodging my own shame, I can so easily slip out of writing plainly and into trying to impress or manipulate readers. I addressed the first draft of this third essay to a fictional "you" who struggles with shame and relationship, and I got to be the teacher-helper. It didn't work. Of course it didn't work. Here, if I don't keep my vulnerable self in the picture, I will have entirely missed the point. I need to remember this as I attempt a plain account of how chronic shame has shaped my capacities for relationship. So, onward.

I wasn't able to count on right-brain (emotional/relational) connection in my childhood, not from my parents or anyone else. Mostly, I just got through my days on my own without much emotion. At home I felt a constant inner murmur of "be careful, be responsible, be good," and then a spike of fear whenever my dad was in a mood. I don't remember anyone being warm, soft, and open to me. In my grade-school years, I didn't have a friend who was a girl. I had no secrets to tell, no feelings to share.

At school, I played sports with the boys, and that worked fine for me. The boys who had baseball gloves would let other kids use their gloves when they were batting. Ronnie always threw his glove to me when he ran in, a dark brown Rawlings made of smooth, supple leather. I loved it and so wished it belonged to me. At recess, I was one of the boys. Inside school I was just a girl who got all the answers right and was no trouble at all. But school was miles away from home, another world. Home was the suburbs of Omaha.

The summer before I turned eight, my parents said I could have a bike for an early birthday present. We went to a store where I chose a blue one with twenty-six-inch wheels, grown-up size. It fit me perfectly and it was smooth and fast. Every day, I rode my bike up and down the long, wide, empty concrete streets of the new housing development, pumping hard on the uphill parts and then sailing down, the wind in my face. I could escape on my bike to an undeveloped part of the suburb where there were some bushes for privacy, a small tree I could climb, and a creek I could follow in both directions for a bit.

Finally, when I was ten, after I had asked politely for years, my mother bought me a yellow leather baseball glove from the department store. It was an ugly colour but it fit my hand right and it wasn't too stiff or heavy. That same day, she bought a small black leather baseball glove for my brother who was only six. He didn't have to wait until he was almost eleven! He didn't have to ask even once!

My six-year-old brother didn't know how to use the glove, and he threw a ball like a girl. I tried to teach him how to catch and throw in the front yard, but in the end I gave up. It worked better for me just to throw a tennis ball hard against the high side of the house where the walkout basement was. The siding would send it off in somewhat unexpected directions, so playing catch with myself was fun there. I could throw the ball hard and field fly balls and one-hoppers for hours.

I see that this isn't about relationships. I guess that's the point. When I was at home and had done my chores, I was on my own to amuse myself. I liked to be out of the house, because the trouble was inside. Besides, if she saw me, my mom could always think of something I could do to help her.

Moving to Mississippi might have given me a better chance to make some friends because there, like everybody else in our new small town, I went to public school. But first I was the new Yankee kid who talked funny. Then, I was the new smart kid, for which I was not bullied, but it didn't make me a lot of friends either. I don't think I noticed. Then I made the basketball team, and I did notice how good it felt to put on a black uniform with bright red numbers front and back and run out there all dressed the same, all-for-one-and-one-for-all, and try to win.

After we'd been there a year, I was turning fourteen and my parents asked me if I would like to invite two friends over for my birthday. Well, not really, but I didn't know how to explain a no. So I chose two girls who played basketball with me, but we weren't really friends. They seemed happy to come, which surprised me. We had pizza and cake and ice cream indoors, and then we shot some baskets in the backyard where my dad had put up my hoop. I tried to chat while we were standing around out there, but I felt awkward. When their parents came to pick them up, I remembered to thank them for coming, but I was relieved it was over. At times like that, I thought there might be something wrong with me.

I was right to wonder what I was missing. I had missed chances to learn basic social engagement behaviours that would help me feel connected to other people, even other kids. But there I was, having my life anyway. I would do my best to work around what I was missing and hide the shame that would fill the empty place. Without noticing, I looked to my parents to show me how to get along with people without having to be really present or emotionally available.

The very first way was to be on a team, of course. My parents were on God's team. I'm not joking. The CRC has all kinds of home mission teams and foreign mission teams. Before they retired, my parents had done both kinds, serving as the quintessential team of minister-and-wife. In the Philippines, late in their career, they travelled to small islands with weekend mission teams that provided basic dentistry along with evangelical films in the local language. Long before, in Omaha days, college students on S.W.I.M. teams (Summer Workshop in Missions) would come for six weeks to live with us, my mom would cook for them, and my dad would be their team leader, teaching them to do outreach and run a two-week Vacation Bible School for kids. We moved to Mississippi so that my dad could be on a team of five young professors eager to start a new seminary.

The second way my parents seemed connected to other people was through their commitment to the beliefs and rituals they shared with others at church. Church members would pray together and sing together, celebrate and mourn together, moved by the same stories and promises, looking upward in faith together. It wasn't looking at one another, but it was the next best thing.

And finally, as minister and wife (not so much as professor and wife), my parents' role was to care for others' spiritual well-being. Their side of the relationship was to offer a particular kind of help, often called "pastoral care." Those who needed such care would bring their emotions along with their needs, but the minister-and-wife team wouldn't bring their own vulnerability to the relationship. The connection was supposed to be asymmetrical, never mutual.

I would gradually take these strategies and make them my own. They would allow me many times of feeling that I belonged with people and had something to offer. But they wouldn't help me learn how to relax and connect. As I moved away from home and into my own life, I saw other people connecting warmly with friends and family, and I knew I couldn't do it. I had never learned how. What I didn't know wasn't trivial. If I didn't know what an open, warm emotional connection felt like, how could I step toward someone hoping to be kindly, warmly welcomed? How could I imagine warmth within me that might feel good to them? I couldn't.

But I'm not going to dismiss the work-arounds I learned from my parents. These strategies for being with others would ease the ache of loneliness and teach me enough relational competence to get along in the world. I think that all sorts of people are doing much that's good and beautiful in the world as they put into play their not-so-vulnerable ways to connect. Their modes of connection – my parents' modes and mine, too – deserve respect and understanding.

Consider what being on a team has to offer. You're valued for your contribution; nobody has to like you for yourself. You do stuff together, and the liking slips in sideways if it's going to. You work side by side, so the question of face-to-face connection doesn't have to come up. You matter to the others because the thing you do together matters.

Planning dates to meet is a group responsibility, so you'll never have to make or break a date personally. You can just count on this connection to be part of your life for a while, but then you can usually get out fairly easily too. Ending with a team is far less complicated than ending a friendship!

There are downsides, however, of counting on teams for connection. Some teams are run by people who just want to get work done and then you end up feeling like a cog in a machine. Teams can breed competition: some people play every game, for example, while some sit on the bench; some people are quiet and some do all the talking in meetings. You or other team members can get caught up in what therapists might call FOO issues (family of origin issues).

FOO issues happen because being on a team for a while can sometimes make you feel like you're back in your original family group. Then your very strategy for keeping relationships uncomplicated lands you in unexpected relational muddles. This can be helpful in a group therapy process: when you start to feel old embodied memories, the group helps you recognize what's happening and integrate it into what you know about yourself. But that's not why you joined this team! Likely nobody here has any idea this sort of thing could happen – for example, that people who were youngest kids could always feel like they have no voice, or that people who were oldest kids would take on too much responsibility and then resent it, or that people who have been bullied or abused will be very suspicious of anyone who takes leadership.

On most teams with specific goals – like setting up a school fair or getting somebody elected – these dynamics can stay quietly under wraps. But where a group demands more personal interaction, troubled interpersonal feelings may emerge. It's good to know that sorting past from present will help you manage your own feelings. It's also important to know that you can't help anyone in your group or team feel better when their trouble has more to do with their past than with what's happening now.

Despite these possible downsides, joining a team can usually be a low-risk way to find interpersonal connection, all the while protecting yourself from the anxieties your chronic shame cranks out. I say this in all seriousness, no tongue in cheek. I have been on countless teams my whole life long because I really do like being with people and ... well, you know the other part of the story.

In my essay about falling apart, I said that life in community didn't meet my longstanding needs for deeper connection. But there's another truth I need to say about those days, too. I would not be who I am today without that community of teamwork, and more specifically without the time I spent in a team of two with Nigel, my husband then. What we had was kinship, a word that also describes how clients with a very tenuous sense of self can begin to find healing connection with therapists. It's the least risky way to connect. It doesn't ask for intense care or even much understanding; it asks only for a response from a place of alikeness. Kinship is how someone begins to come in out of the cold, trying to find another human so that they can feel less alien.

W. Eugene Smith took a photograph in 1946 that he called "The Walk to Paradise Garden." I have brought my framed copy of it with me to every therapy office I've used over the decades. Once Nigel stopped by the office and looked at the print for a long minute. "That's us, you know." I could suddenly see what he saw. Yes, there we are, two very small children trudging sturdily side by side, out of darkness and toward a sunny forest clearing.

Much of our kinship was unconscious. We both came from families where pain, blame, and shame were inflicted, suffered, resented, and never talked about plainly, much less worked through, families whose legacy was chronic shame. And so we each brought deep vulnerabilities along with considerable gifts to our relationship. The other's vulnerability didn't frighten us because we each knew the alien within ourselves. In retrospect, I'd say the deal was this: not to tread on vulnerability, which would keep our own vulnerability safe; or to put it another way: at a deep level to cause no further shame.

This allowed us to live a life of kinship, doing grad school on a shoestring, having children and caring for them, taking them hiking, camping, and swimming with us, reading library books to them and listening to folk music on the radio, shopping, cooking, and cleaning, doing our co-op and church things, trading back and forth years of working and years of going back to school, becoming less and less alien, finding a place in the world. We did remarkable work as a team.

In my younger years, joining teams let me connect when being with others heart to heart wasn't something I knew how to do very well. And then sometimes when I was doing my best to contribute to a team, being my best self for the group, something else would happen. I would see and be seen face-to-face anyway in moments that felt to me like accidents, like random grace. But the grace became reliable. Today the friends I trust most deeply with my heart were teammates first – learning partners, teaching partners, business partners, and yes, Nigel too, who is no longer partner but friend.

For this reason as well, teams are worth doing. If they're your thing. I suppose teams have been my thing because my family of origin felt like a team when it was running smoothly. And what team wouldn't welcome a capable, reliable big sister who can tolerate a bumpy ride and get things done?

But for me, connecting wasn't just about joining teams to get things done. I had watched my parents looking upward with fellow believers, and I had looked upward too. The groups I joined in early adulthood were passionate about a certain religious world-and-life view and principles of social justice. Later in life, my passion turned toward understanding how relational psychotherapy works its deep, subtle changes and what it takes to become a therapist who can join people in that process. For twenty-seven years, I belonged to a faculty team committed to a project bigger than ourselves. We read theory, created curriculum, taught, supervised, and led intensive group process, working our way through countless entanglements of students' relational traumas, often by putting ourselves in the line of fire – and all in service of learning how one becomes a self capable of facilitating powerful, safe therapeutic relationships.

It was something we marvelled at, teachers and students alike, on graduation evenings: the remarkable and often surprising growth unique to each graduate and so visible now, change that had been driven by four or five years of a learning process that was often as gruelling as it was enlightening. We had lived this training program together, a way for theory to become gut instinct, and while we came to know each other well in those trenches, we were also connected by our commitment to the thing we had created, the embodiment of a vision.

Many things that humans create can be powerful points of connection even when the meeting isn't face to face. Aesthetic experiences and objects of art mediate interpersonal intensity. Dancers, actors, and musicians connect with their audience by way of a third thing that they bring to life. Artists put into the world something of themselves that is distilled and crafted beyond simple presence, and therein lies its power. A gifted teacher draws a student into a passionate relationship with ideas, something between them that enlivens them both. Landscape architects and home renovators, goat breeders and dog trainers, gardeners and bakers – they all connect with us, and we with them, through what they do.

I've enjoyed this kind of connection in writing and teaching. I know what it feels like to connect over something I have crafted with passion, and I also know what it feels like simply to connect, person to person, in moments of soft, warm openness. I'm not saying here that one experience is better than the other; I'm just passing on a tip. I've found that if I'm feeling too scared or shy or inept to move toward somebody simply to connect, I can still say (if not in so many words): "I won't ask you to see me, but please see what moves me, what I've made, what I've discovered. Be with me this way." The satisfaction in this kind of connection is genuine and reliable.

Giving and receiving care is another kind of connection that doesn't require much risky mutual presence. When this kind of connection works well, both parties stay in a role, but that doesn't make the connection false. There is real vulnerability in sharing one's troubles or in accepting care. There is real presence in listening deeply or in giving emotional or physical care with kindness. At the same time, the relationship is asymmetrical, not mutual, not really face to face.

Like my parents before me, I decided to make a career out of asymmetrical relationships. I would create safe space for people to be vulnerable enough to get the help they needed from me. Safety would mean, in part, that I wouldn't bring my own personal need for connection into the space. That was just fine with me, since I couldn't show up in person very well anyway. I could concentrate on learning how to attune to my clients' emotions and show empathy, a task I understood from being a parent.

In my training, I was warned about a trickier way I might use my role to meet my own needs: I might see my needy self in the people I was helping, and then my taking care of them would actually be a sneaky way to take care of myself. Now I can see the chronic shame this situation would disguise: disowning my own neediness, my own hunger to connect, as shameful, yet being pulled to connect with vulnerable needy people to assuage their shame and thus assuage my own. I didn't know about disguised shame then; I just knew that my hunger to connect belonged to me, and so I stayed in my own personal therapy, with the side benefit that my clients would be protected from my unfinished personal business.

Given who I am, what a strange thing I do for a living! When I quit my Ph.D. and told my friend Henk, in the hallway of the Institute for Christian Studies, that I was going to be a therapist instead of an academic, he looked at me as if he were choking back some words. Henk was too old to be my big brother, too young to be a father figure. He was also a *bona fide* Christian philosopher and on the preaching team with me. Finally he said what was stuck in his throat: "Most people try to maximize their strengths when they choose a career!" Later, when I was a therapist and he found himself in his own therapy (a time which cemented our friendship), he apologized for what he had said those years before. I told him he was right: I'd headed directly toward my weakness. By then he understood that sometimes that's what you have to do.

What is this thing I do for a living? I offer consistent emotional presence, right-brain attunement, ventral vagal presence – all those things I missed so much as a kid, all those things not available to me to absorb and carry into my own relational life, all those things I have had to learn painstakingly like learning to speak a second language or how to swim in adulthood. My offer of presence is sincere, heartfelt. At the same time, it comes from inside my role and for a therapeutic reason: to make therapy a place where trust and attachment can happen.

Attachment may stir up childhood feelings for a client, especially of need and shame, and then the therapy relationship becomes more complicated. I'm there for that. I understand what's happening. A good therapy outcome depends on working through these feelings openly. My client may now insist that I "be there for real" – engaged in the struggle, expressing genuine feelings. I will do my best work if I'm as emotionally honest as possible – *in their best interests.* The rules of unconditional empathy and "inflict no shame" still hold.

Thus, though I intentionally offer warm understanding, and though my best work is done when I show up for real, none of this is to satisfy my need for personal connection. I'm always asking myself what kind of being-with would best meet my client's need right now. Sometimes meeting a need just now and just right drops into a place of mutual understanding, of seeing and being seen, a moment that's tender and sweet or sad or funny. But I don't seek it or expect it. Such moments of grace just happen sometimes.

In summary, let me emphasize that these ways of relating that I learned from my parents – working on teams, sharing beliefs and commitments, caring for others – are not second-best ways to connect. On the contrary, each of them takes some time to learn to do well. Each embodies a kind of grace – the grace of kinship and belonging, the grace of creative expression and passions shared, the grace of giving and receiving. Each kind of grace is a constellation of energy where the power of love in the universe meets human need and desire, inviting us to come more fully out of isolated shame and into loving connection.

Nevertheless, in all these activities, these things to do and to share, there are sometimes only very few moments of knowing and being known face to face, heart to heart. What I still always long for, quietly, patiently, is to connect in that open, soft, warm way with another human being I know and love, nothing to accomplish together, nothing to create, no one to take care of.

Deep, lasting friendships may be the best kind of open-hearted relationships to pursue. Friends don't have to manage the complexities of sexual desire or the responsibilities of making a life together. But if I'm discussing shame and relationships, I'll have to include sexual pair-bonding relationships. That's because most of us look for reliable heart-to-heart connection in this kind of primary relationship. But shame also wreaks much havoc here.

Let me put on my therapist hat for a bit to describe how this works, or often doesn't work.

When couples carry in their bodies histories of unsafe relationships, right-brain resonance between them will be powerful but incoherent. Their two nervous systems will rarely be able to rest in a safe ventral vagal mode and enjoy the simple reassuring pleasures of hugs, affection, and kindness. With their fight-or-flight nervous systems often activated, they will spend more and more time in reactive anger or protective shutdown because they have no safe place of return.

That's why my work with couples mired in blame and shame always begins with empathy and affect regulation. I listen carefully to each of them in turn, reflecting their emotions and encouraging them to clarify or elaborate. As I listen and respond, I try to embody safety, openness, warmth. I hope their bodies can relax and that their right brains can feel my presence with them. I hope that the one who isn't talking with me in the moment will see how I try to be soft and accepting with their partner, that they will notice that this changes the feeling of the conversation, if ever so slightly.

If neither of them can stop blaming the other for the trouble between them, I'll guess that they each brought a load of shame into this relationship. I can imagine their disappointments ever since. Falling in love would have felt miraculous; being seen as wonderful is a powerful antidote to shame. Unconditional love provides euphoric relief from the emotional isolation at the heart of shame. The more shame and inner emptiness a couple brings to their relationship, the higher their hopes will be that love will cure them, and then, sadly, the more bruising their disillusionment will be. If their partner complains or criticizes them, they fall from feeling special to feeling worthless. If their partner fails to tune into what they need, they feel utterly alone and unloved.

What a terrible thing falling in love can be, as all the sad songs say. This love has opened each of them to hurt they hadn't felt before – or not that they can remember. In fact, feeling this pain now is their remembering, their making contact with a helpless, shamed neediness they shut down long ago. We are back to where chronic shame started, and it is, indeed, a very painful place.

This is as bad as it gets for couples, and sometimes it doesn't get better. Their shame may keep them from knowing what's going on. It's just too hard to feel the want and rage that's rising up in them, too humiliating to own their longing and hurt. The fights always come back to the same question: *Why won't you be who I want you to be and love me the way I want to be loved?* The question is an accusation, each shaming the other, and so their deep longing for a healing, restorative love will never be met. The trauma that produces chronic shame just repeats itself.

Meanwhile, if they keep coming (in spite of themselves and because they have no hope elsewhere), I gently stop the accusations and ask them to talk to me about how they feel inside, what's going on for them. I keep listening to each and responding with empathy and understanding. Slowly, slowly, something may start to soften, not because of any new ideas in the room, but because I keep insisting on and inviting them into interpersonal safety with me.

If the therapy room at last becomes a relatively safe space for each of them, I will offer to help them learn to do this with each other: listen, try to understand with empathy, and then reflect accurately what the other person is trying to say. I will help them take turns giving and receiving these safe messages. I will coach lightly, translate sometimes, and stay ready to step in with some calm understanding should someone get dysregulated.

While we're doing this work, I will tell them that what they talk about together is not nearly as important as how they talk about it. By making things safer, we're trying to change the *how* from something defensively tight to something more open and friendly. I ask them what they have seen in their lives about how relationships work. I know that if they have lived mostly in systems of chronic shame, there will be so much they never had a chance to learn.

For example, if making a mistake means that they're totally wrong, making an apology just invites further humiliation. They don't expect their partner to honour their apology and affirm them as a good, loveable person. They also have no idea how to receive an apology kindly, with care for their partner's vulnerability in offering it. They will need to experience these strange, new, but safe interactions over and over until they can access them to use under stress. But as things start to move in a calmer, more reliable direction, fight-and-flight energy eases and the couple's capacity to be vulnerable and fallible with each other grows.

This sounds like a pedestrian achievement: "We went to therapy and learned how to have a conversation instead of a fight." But given the fear, rage, and despair emotional intimacy brings up in people who suffer chronic shame, it's actually a remarkable achievement. The experience of being deeply understood in one's emotions, not only by one's therapist but also by one's partner, changes everything. A "needy" longing for love does not have to be a shameful secret. Need is honoured instead and met with compassion and respect. Here and now, the trauma of chronic shame, the annihilation of vulnerability, does not have to repeat itself.

These couples now have a chance to be brave enough and steady enough to care for their own and their partner's woundedness. It's awful when shamed vulnerabilities from old relationships come back to life in a new relationship. But it's also a chance to open up to radical change. None of this change comes without struggle, but there is hard-earned beauty and grace in the struggle, the beauty of being honest and present, the grace of surrendering to what has been true and of hoping for something different. Paradoxically, this grace specializes in broken hearts, in not being able to get it right the first time, and in never being perfect. It's about becoming more whole in relationship by way of becoming open to pain … and then coming through to some joy and peace. It's never about completion.

———————

I was not open to facing difficult emotions in my first marriage. Nor was my husband, as far as I could tell. Since our deal was to protect our own vulnerabilities and to cause each other no further shame, we had very little room to negotiate differences, or even to notice differences. Thus the shame that shut us down inside our solitudes was never addressed.

I didn't expect Nigel to give me the love I had missed in my childhood. I didn't hate him for failing to love me perfectly. Our relationship did not access those dissociated longings in me. But then, as I eventually came to know, I hadn't fallen in love with him, though I trusted and loved him as a friend and partner. I also never sensed frustrated desire in him for deep connection he had missed out on, and so I wonder whether he actually fell in love with me. Looking back, I sense that my competence and stability made him feel safe in the world, that my everyday trust and love gave him a platform from which to operate, and that was good enough.

We were more "kin" than lovers, and this structure of relationship kept us side by side, looking toward the project of adulthood we were trying to manage together. We rarely looked at each other to wonder, "What's going on for you inside?" We rarely squared off face to face to ask for some sort of change from the other. I remember trying twice to address straightforwardly the "household chores" issue, the bane of many unions. I remember getting what I thought was an honest response: "I don't see dirt. I'm not going to change. So if that's what you want, I guess we're stuck."

In the end, my solution was to suggest that Nigel do the shopping and cooking, chores he could "see" and mostly enjoy, and I would do the cleaning and laundry. I didn't like cleaning either, but it was an arrangement I could accept without major resentment. Minor resentment wasn't worth thinking about, especially if there was no hope of change. For all our side-by-side kinship, I often experienced Nigel as quite closed off to me, in his own world of interests and preferences he assumed I shared. He may have experienced me to be just as self-absorbed and closed off to him. In truth, I think that neither of us knew what we were missing of face-to-face, heart-to-heart connection.

In retrospect, I understand his "I'm not going to change" as a defence against entering a conflictual conversation. Nigel brought from his family of origin the certainty that conflict cannot be worked through. His father was just despicably wrong and his mother was just terribly ill-treated, and nothing could be done to make anything better. In fact, any kind of talking would bring only shame and despair to the surface. Best to choose your position and not be budged. My own family history had left me with a visceral fear of unresolvable conflict, so the last thing I wanted to do was to push us into our own shame/blame spiral.

If my sexual orientation hadn't become a spanner in the works, we might have stayed together and found a way to transform our solid working partnership into more genuine emotional connectedness. We would have needed to be honest about our angers and disappointments, clear about what we wanted and needed from each other. We would have had to look into each other's faces and feel scary, destabilizing emotions. We might have ended one kind of marriage and begun another, as some people do.

But that didn't happen because we were "kin" for a reason. The kind of sexual and emotional bonding we would have needed to carry us through such a long, arduous process of relational growth just wasn't there. There was no second marriage available to us that would have made the struggle worthwhile.

"Well," you might ask, "Where's the grace in that story?" That's a fair question. Honest, vulnerable relationship undoes the power of shame, but before Nigel and I separated, we hadn't had a chance to come through to that kind of openness. We hadn't even begun to face the shame that had locked us down, and so we could not begin to loosen its bonds. You might say that shame won that round.

On the other hand, we kept the worst of it at bay. We created the most honest, loving relationship we could manage. Our capacities to self-regulate emotion by shutting it down spared us having to deal with out-of-control feelings. Our tacit refusal to set off the landmines of shame and blame that lay beneath conflict was the best way we knew to protect ourselves and our children from the pain we had witnessed and endured as children. I want to honour our effort. For every couple who is able to manage the full process of facing and disempowering shame together, there must be scores of couples whose bond endures because of creative work-arounds and unspoken agreements not to poke the bear.

This too is a kind of grace in an imperfect world. In the vision I choose to believe, in which a force for love in the universe is both full of grief and persistent in hope, nobody gets it right the first time, or perhaps ever. When we do the best we can and then look back across the years to critical times that feel like failure, we can be kind to our younger striving selves and say, as I said to myself on a windy country road this spring, *It's okay. You were doing what you could with what you knew. What you did got us here, and now, going forward, there can be more healing and wholeness, maybe even joy.*

At the same time, it would be dishonest to downplay the damage done. Some of what remained unsaid between Nigel and me became passive-aggressive behaviour, amplifying anxiety in the family. Some of our unspoken hurt went underground as our contribution to a multi-generational legacy of chronic shame which has now been passed to our children. There's no making that okay. There's just going forward with hope tempered by a measure of regret and sorrow.

———————

That wasn't the end of the story. We all did go forward. As adults, our kids haven't been afraid to search for and work on meaningful relationships of honest emotional presence – and honest struggle, if need be. My story continued with Mary, most of which I have yet to tell. Nigel and his wife Jean created a partnership of much mutual understanding and enduring love. Nigel and I collaborated as parents during the years when our kids alternated living a week with Mary and me and a week with him and Jean. When the kids left home, Nigel and Jean moved to Maritime Canada, and they worked there until their retirement as United Church clergy. Then they moved back to Toronto, and we resumed friendly connection like extended family.

We had been in our respective relationships with our new partners for nearly three decades by the time the pandemic hit. As everyone did, I hunkered down at home in isolation with the person who shared home with me. Few people knew that Mary was slowly slipping into a subtle but disabling dementia. She always recognized me and understood whatever was happening in the moment, but increasing blanks in her short-term memory left her bewildered and frightened. She became unable to do her own banking and correspondence, to remember the day of the week or whether she had eaten her lunch.

If Mary had been able to continue to socialize with friends and play bridge weekly, we could have staved off the disabling effects of the dementia for a while. But as it was, one day she decided that there was no point getting up, getting dressed, and coming downstairs. She would just stay in bed. I couldn't coax her into changing her mind. Getting downstairs and up again with a cane and a chairlift was hard work for her, with no immediate payoff. I could understand that. Upstairs she had her comfortable ensuite bathroom. Her TV was full of recorded shows and golf tournaments, favourites she could watch again and again. And so I adjusted. We had our meals together upstairs in the bedroom.

Since the pandemic meant that I suddenly had to work virtually, I tried for a while to work from home. But Mary couldn't stop interrupting me. She fully understood, every time I reminded her, that therapy sessions weren't supposed to be interrupted. But she would forget where I was and what I was doing, and then she couldn't stop herself from calling out for me or coming to find me.

Eventually I rented an office a short walk from home, from which I did virtual sessions four days a week. We had personal service workers come in for a few hours weekly when I was away. The days I left home, I would leave yogurt and fresh berries on her bedside table, a lunch sandwich wrapped up nearby, cookies in a tin. Evenings, at her request, we had the soups she most liked me to make and ice cream for dessert, and then we'd watch the news and a rerun of one of the Britcoms whose plot she could follow. Or not follow, but at least we were doing something together.

I felt trapped, sad, and lonely in our isolation – but who didn't in those days? As the pandemic eased, we were able to travel to the lakehouse, a place where there were only a few level steps between her bed and her living room chair, where birds came to feeders on the windows, big windows that opened onto sun shining through the trees and across the lake. For that, Mary would get up out of bed, dressed, into the car, and then, at the end, up the four steps to the lakehouse porch, quite a feat of determination and grit.

There at the lakehouse, once it became pandemic-safe to do so, Nigel and Jean came to spend a weekend with us. On the last full day, after Mary had gone to bed, they asked me to sit down with them at the table to talk. They asked how I was doing and I tried to be truthful. "I'm okay ... and it's hard."

They said they could see that it was hard and lonely and that I was wearing down. They said they had a proposal for me. They wanted to come over to the condo late Monday afternoons while I would be still at work. Jean would chat with Mary and walk the dog while Nigel would make dinner. On that one day of every week, I would have nothing to do but come home – without rushing – and be looked after, and I would have company and real conversation.

I resisted their offer at first. Their kindness shone a light on my weariness and need, which felt shameful to me. And it was such an unexpectedly generous offer; how could I ever reciprocate? But they emphasized that this was what they *wanted* to do: it would make them happy. They suggested that we try it for just a week or two.

A week or two became many months. Mary wanted only her favourite soups from me, but she became very fond of any Monday meal featuring a tender meat, mashed potatoes, and gravy, so we ate that often, along with lovely vegetables she wouldn't touch. The three of us treasure the memories of sitting in that bedroom with plates in our laps, wineglasses on random safe surfaces, chatting about things Mary could follow, creating in that otherwise lonely space the warmth of communion. I know that's true because we have said so to one another other lately, eating a meal together at the farm.

How is it that we are eating meals together at a farm? That's another story, and I'll tell it briefly. As Mary's physical and mental condition deteriorated, I knew we could not go on as we were. But I couldn't face finding an assisted living situation for her in the city of Toronto. I learned that good spaces were in very short supply, and we would have to be "flexible." I imagined how abandoned she would feel in a faraway part of the city. I knew that I would want to be with her as often as I could. But that would mean fighting congested roads or transit every day between home or work and whatever decent residence I could find for her.

I began to cast about for a creative solution. Ninety minutes from downtown Toronto, I found a six-acre plot of rural land for sale with an almost-finished bungalow on it, built to be accessible. Most importantly, up a country road just four minutes away, there was a five-star private seniors' residence, with views over Lake Huron's Georgian Bay. It included floors for assisted living and memory-care living. They would have room for her, and Mary was deemed appropriate for their care. I bought the property in the fall, and we moved the next spring, after the winter of our Monday night meals with Nigel and Jean.

My plan was to work virtually from this "farm" two days a week and drive to the city to see clients in person two other days, staying over one night. On the days I was working at the farm, trips up the hill to spend time with Mary would be quick and easy. Friday mornings until Sunday evenings, I could bring her down any time or all the time to our accessible new home in the country, where she could see gardens put in and birdfeeders put up. And getting to the lakehouse would be a shorter, easier trip, too.

We did get to the lakehouse for a few weekends, and I brought Mary down to the farm for some sunny summer afternoons. She wasn't comfortable staying longer. As it turned out, her health was failing more quickly than I had thought it would. Four months after our move, she was in the local hospital for five weeks. Less than two months later, she was admitted again with a sepsis that turned into general system failure and her final move into palliative care.

All this time Nigel and Jean were standing by – quite literally, because they were staying at the farm two days a week. When I bought it, I invited them to consider living part-time there and helping to turn it from weedy meadows with scattered trees into whatever we might imagine. I knew they'd had dreams of finding their own land, but that the pandemic exodus to "the country" had put Maritime prices out of reach for them. This would at least get their feet out of the city and into some soil. Also, since I was still working and caring for Mary, not to mention nearing seventy, I knew I'd never develop a garden property on my own.

Nigel and Jean were eager to embark on the experiment, a stab at something new for life after seventy. They also imagined that their time at the farm would include helping me care for Mary – re-instating our Monday night dinners on Fridays, perhaps, and being around for some overnights. But she was never well enough to participate; in the late afternoons, I always left the farm to spend time with her at the residence or hospital.

That time of giving care has now passed, and we are still here, sharing meals at the farm together and with kids and grandkids, too, on some weekends. I still work four days a week, two in the city. Nigel and Jean each have part-time contract work with churches in the city. Our gardens are taking shape slowly. How this evolves over time remains to be seen. But that's not the point here. This essay is about shame and relationship – how shame blocks emotional intimacy, and how relationships shut down by shame have to open themselves to vulnerability before they can open to heart-to-heart connection. I was saying that Nigel and I never had a chance to go through that process together. But now we do.

The truth is that no matter how modestly we envision our farm project or how intermittently we share the space, Nigel and I are going to have to learn to do our inevitable conflicts openly and respectfully, face to face. For all our kindnesses given and received, we can't avoid the other side of relationship. When conflict happens, we will still have to go through our shamed vulnerabilities to get to honest connection. Sometimes grace is relentless.

You would think that after thirty years of living with other partners in other circles of friends, gaining the wisdom and maturity that should come with age, we would be able to do this. But old habits die hard. The old shame lurks; the old self-protections are tenacious. Jean wisely leaves us to work it out on our own. At least we know enough to expect something better of ourselves.

After one Friday morning flare-up and then a long icy shutdown, I know enough to get over myself and make the first move. I ask Nigel, "What's going on for you?" He knows enough to overcome his pained silence (which I feel as punishing) and explain what I have done to undermine him and hurt his feelings. I understand and apologize, but then I also defend my reactivity and my intentions. I add that I have been hurt too – by hours of that silence.

Nigel says, "We do both hate to be in the wrong!" Yes, there's the shame. Neither of us can be reactive, hurtful, petty, stubborn, and then feel genuinely sorry and truly forgiven and come back easily to a sustaining sense of being a good, loveable person – who sometimes acts badly but would rather not. Shame says: *You can't come back; there's* no real repair. *That good, loveable person is wiped out. You won't be forgiven for real, so there's no point in saying sorry for real.*

On this Friday, I'm glad Nigel has called out the shame. I tell him I agree with him; we both do hate to be in the wrong. But I would rather have had a simple apology from him. He was saying, I think, that he would have preferred a simple apology from me. Yet this is far better than it was. I'd also say – if I were writing a report card for us – that improvement is needed. The report assumes improvement is possible.

Many Fridays later, and not long after I wrote the words *improvement is possible*, I shared an early version of these essays with Nigel. I thought that he might want me to say some things differently, but I didn't expect him to feel terribly hurt on reading what I wrote. My mistake, born of our history of wordless kinship, was to assume that he held our past in the same way I did. Something in how I brought up the memories set off deep, disorienting pain in him. I had blundered into another chance at getting through hurt and shame to honesty and reconnection. I felt badly about what I had done. But there we were.

Nigel took the time he needed to come to understand his hurt and grief, and then he asked to talk. I was able to hear his pain and respond with care and sorrow for having hurt him. He refused to blame me; he used his disorientation to reassess what he really wanted to do about his continuing life in ministry and his slice of life on the farm. And he asked me if we might schedule a few sessions with a therapist where he could have a chance to say some things he never had a chance to feel clearly, much less to say, those many years ago when we separated.

Yes. I do want to join him in such a meeting, and I will be open to whatever it will mean for me. The "improvements" in the speaking and hearing we need to do are not beyond our reach. At seventy and seventy-one, we can still rewrite the legacies of shame we were born into.

And sometimes, it's simpler than we imagine. We have learned over the last year or so that if either of us feels misunderstood, it's good practice to take time out for a coffee or a beer in the town five minutes away, a chance to sit across a table from each other, face to face, and talk. And listen. There we can rediscover how to be old friends who can now enjoy some ventral vagal safety and right-brain connection with each other – in spite of and because of all that's gone down. We can be grateful for the grace of second chances.

Relationship, as it embodies the energy of love in the universe, is always creating second chances for healing and growth, and more chances beyond that. I choose to believe this. I know, however, that the energy of hate is just as potent, destroying relationship in endless cycles of fear, shame, and rage that lead to nothing but isolation and despair.

In the Judeo-Christian myth of human origins, Eden is like a remembered dream. The knowledge of good and evil defines the waking life humans have been thrown into. Knowing good and evil, our first parents also felt their shameful, naked vulnerability. They had to bend their bodies to the brutally hard work of surviving and reproducing. When their two sons became men and put the fruits of their labours before God, Abel's offering found favour, but Cain's did not. Cain's face and spirit fell. In the Genesis story, God came to him and said, in essence, "You don't need to be angry. You know how to make this better between us." But Cain didn't do the work to make it better. Instead, in his shame and rage, he called Abel out into a field for a talk and killed him there.

Reflecting on the history and current state of the earth, we might agree that this, too, is an essential story of who we are as humans. We are all implicated in legacies of self-aggrandizement and heartless violence. This story of origin may also fit our personal experience of relationship better than any imagined Eden of secure attachment and open, warm connectedness. Even if no one got killed in our childhood families, there's still blood in the ground and the curse of lonely shame; there's no experience of repair, no remorse or forgiveness.

And yet somehow, we've also found ways to move on from childhood and toward relationship. The lure of connection, with maybe a chance at healing, has caught us in spite of our fears. And now here we are, having hurt someone we care about, having been hurt. Can we bear to face what we've done and speak what we feel? Or has everything gone murderous again? Will we come out forgiving and forgiven or humiliated? If we're walking survivors of endless relational destruction, we can only expect more isolation and shame. How could we ever learn to say "I'm sorry," trusting we'll be loved, or "I forgive you," trusting that we'll lose nothing?

Such conversation can happen only among bodies that are safe with each other. We've come full circle, back to polyvagal basics. Having a difference with someone is safe only when there is no hostile shaming energy coming at us or emanating from our own bodies, when instead there is mutual respect and care within which difference can be negotiated. We can't create this safety on our own. We can't create it for someone who approaches with hostility. We have to create it together. Making conflict safer is always a joint achievement, and it may well take a third person, or a community, to hold and calm the hostile shaming energy until some mutual empathy can be found, the foundation of respect and care.

The skills of conflict resolution won't work without some emotional openness between the people in conflict. Learning empathy is more strenuous and complicated than learning skills, but it's worth the try, over and over. If we can feel into the other's pain instead of our own shame, our apology will be genuine. We will also be able to accept an apology from them simply, no further recriminations, when we remember, "I've made mistakes, too, and I've needed forgiveness."

Shame is the enemy of conflict resolution, and thus the enemy of relationship, because it won't let us think clearly about our failures, much less make them right. It seems that after the first failed offering, Cain might have said to God, "I'm sorry I didn't get that right. Let me try again." The story suggests that if he had accepted his failure with humility and willingness to change, he would have found acceptance. Instead, feeling small in his shame, he did something to make himself feel large and strong again. To silence his shame, he murdered his brother.

In this story of origins, a prototypical, irreparable evil act has its roots in the shame that one human did not master. What is it to "master" shame? Shame itself tells us, once we have felt the sting of failure, the disgrace of losing out, that owning our frailty will only make us feel far, far worse. We're sure that to master this shame we must make ourselves invincible and eliminate whatever threatens us. We don't know that this will send us wandering the face of the earth in disowned chronic shame, briefly invincible perhaps, but alien and alone.

True mastery of shame lies in the opposite direction. Accepting the shame of our faults and limitations is the only way to arrive at peace with who we actually are. Mastery of shame is accepting what we find shameful in ourselves with sturdy, accountable self-compassion, not self-recrimination. Compassion for all parts of ourselves allows us a reliable depth of compassion for others. Mastering shame by accepting what's real about ourselves is the only way for us to live in peaceable connection with fellow travellers who struggle as we do to live kindly and well for a few years on this earth.

Owning vulnerability is also the only way to enter conflictual situations with respect and care for others as well as for ourselves. The alternative is a battle of hostile shaming energy, each party determined to make the other totally wrong so that no wrong can be laid at their door. Mutual violent retaliation becomes "righteous," and then the conflict can never be resolved, whether the war is within a family or between nations. Third parties despair of helping such antagonists admit to their own shamed vulnerability and the harms they have perpetrated to cover it up.

Sometimes, antagonists are not equally matched. In the long history of one powerful group of humans doing violent harm to another less powerful group, some hope has recently emerged. Visionaries have come to believe that reconciliation may be possible here – but only by way of truth. This truth is spoken by one oppressed, broken heart at a time, telling of harm done for which there is no excuse. Listeners ask themselves to be present with their own hearts, to acknowledge their complicity in systemic denials of this truth, and to seek ways to repair harms done. Any such truth and reconciliation process undertakes a massive confrontation of shame, I believe, both survivor shame and perpetrator shame, and when the process fails, I believe it's because shame wins. Very often it's because those of us who profit from past and present oppression can't bear the shame of knowing the harm done or of knowing how we resist what repair would ask of us.[3]

When we despair of change in the big picture – of factions and nations ever laying down arms, of an oppressor group ever offering reparative justice to those it oppresses – it may help to remember that reconciliation is a process that happens when one shamed heart makes connection with another shamed heart despite generations of terrible pain between them. We each have so little power to influence the grand scheme of things. Perhaps the power of love in the universe doesn't have such grand or global influence either, only the power to draw human hearts, one at a time, toward openness and connection. Its only power is love, after all. But two hearts in connection can become four, and then eight people sturdy in their fallible humanity, sixteen people passionate to stop harm and repair what's broken. Thirty-two make a group, and sixty-four start a movement whose energy still moves from heart to heart. Maybe that's how it works: infinite tiny points of grace ripple outward, becoming waves that join up to become powerful surges of change toward a greater good.

My experience of struggle and grace is one of those tiny points, and yours is another. The energy that flashes at their point of meeting belongs to us but also to a power that calls us to respond with lovingkindness to others and accountability for the choices we make in relationship.

On the ground where I live my tiny slice of life and make my choices, I know that conflict will always be with me. I will keep making mistakes and getting stung myself. My goal is resilience, not perfection. I want to carry my imperfection comfortably, with a sense of humour and a quick willingness to make amends. I want to trust relationship enough to keep coming back to connection through whatever shamed vulnerability lies between me and someone I love. Sometimes it will take work-arounds, good-enoughs, not giving up though never getting it right. But what choice do I have if I want to be here and be-with?

What choice do any of us have? "Here" is a world where generosity and greed constantly compete for our alliance. Perhaps our knowledge of good and evil is not a curse, just a description of our deepest challenge as humans, one we would like to escape but cannot. We always have to choose, and our choices have consequences. We need to know the harm we do as clearly as we know the good. On a larger scale, we must not turn away from the harm humans do egregiously all around us, and with our systemic participation. And then what will we choose to do?

It seems naïve even to me that I recommend love, with reference to a power of love in the universe that may be only wishful thinking. But on the other hand, if things are going to change for the better, hearts will have to change first. They change one at a time. And the only heart I have to work with is my own. More and more, I can feel the goodness of safe, heartfelt human connection. I know how compassionate presence restores well-being. I accept parts of myself that cause me shame. I have come to value kindness, respect, fairness, and compassion above all virtues. What I can do is this: tell you how the challenges of heart-to-heart relationship have changed my heart for the better, and hope that my sparks of grace might connect with yours and then join up with waves of light and warmth that can still make a difference in a brutal world.

As humans, we are still wired to seek out connectedness with other humans when our fears and defences subside. If we can be touched by the warmth of connection, even our wounded, guarded hearts may still be inspired to move with the power of love – to turn away from brutality and destruction and toward compassion and hope renewed.

NOTES

1 Stephen W. Porges, The Pocket Guide to the Polyvagal Theory: The Transformative Power of Feeling Safe (New York: Norton, 2017).

2 See Stephen W. Porges and Deb A. Dana, eds., Clinical Applications of the Polyvagal Theory: The Emergence of Polyvagal-Informed Therapies (New York: Norton, 2018).

3 See Patricia DeYoung, "Societies of Chronic Shame," in Understanding and Treating Chronic Shame: Healing Right Brain Relational Trauma, 2nd ed. (New York: Routledge, 2021), 101–134.

REFERENCES

DeYoung, Patricia. Understanding and Treating Chronic Shame: Healing Right Brain Relational Trauma, 2nd ed. New York: Routledge, 2021.

Porges, Stephen W. The Pocket Guide to the Polyvagal Theory: The Transformative Power of Feeling Safe. New York: Norton, 2017.

Porges, Stephen W., and Deb A. Dana, eds. Clinical Applications of the Polyvagal Theory: The Emergence of Polyvagal-Informed Therapies. New York: Norton, 2018.

Essay Four

I once consulted a psychoanalyst who had a tidy dark beard, smooth black eyebrows, and quiet brown eyes that gave nothing away. After our six assessment sessions, he told me that he didn't think it would be wise for us to continue into psychoanalysis. His explanation: "I notice that your eyes track me closely, never looking away. I don't think you want analysis. I think you want forgiveness."

Forgiveness for what? I didn't think to ask. If we had continued, I would have had to work through a relationship with my father and every other authority who had assumed knowledge about me. Though I was relieved to be let off the hook, I was also chagrined. I wasn't good enough for psychoanalysis because I wanted something I shouldn't want. "Forgiveness" wasn't quite right; I knew that. But I also knew that he had seen something close to the bone in me. I wouldn't want him to direct an impersonal analysis of my psyche; I would want something *from him*. He thought it would be forgiveness.

If he felt that my interpersonal wanting was wrong, and it seemed he did, I'd need his forgiveness for that. I did not want to go there. This was not my first or even my third therapy. I went on from there to spend years with a self psychology analyst who was committed to understanding me from inside my experience, and that was close enough to where I wanted to go. Even so, I wanted too much from him, but at least I didn't crash and burn with the humiliation of desire. Empathy made for softer landings.

Humiliated desire for what? What did I want, always? I wanted to be totally present in my passionately feeling self and to be received with kindness, interest, energy, reciprocity, joy. I wanted all my wants to be okay, whether or not they could be met. I wanted intense mutual engagement, and I wanted to feel safely and quietly held. I wanted what I didn't have words for yet – ventral vagal availability for soft, warm connection; lively right-brain state-sharing and communion.

DOI: 10.4324/9781003499121-4

I wanted what every newborn is getting ready to want insistently from her people, and what every lonely, silenced child is looking for at the end of some rainbow.

On the one hand, there's absolutely nothing wrong with that bundle of want, nothing to forgive. On the other hand, there's not a psychotherapy on the planet that can satisfy it.

You're not born knowing what you want, but you learn it fast. If all goes well, your sense of "I want" should intensify as you get to be two and three. Then it will need to be modulated for the sake of sociability, but never squashed. Your particular wants are what make you the little person that you are. Why should you lose them? If you're safe with your people, you can want what you want and ask for it. Maybe even stomp and pout a bit. They'll love you anyway, they'll tell you what the limits are, and you'll adjust. The optimistic principle of "It can't hurt to ask" makes wanting a hopeful, even cheerful state of being.

But what if you're not safe with your people because they aren't safe in themselves? Then keeping safe becomes your primary want. If asking rocks the boat, you won't want to ask. Also, you might not be sure that your people will love you anyway if you ask for what you want. Making sure that they love you, or are at least pleased with you, becomes another primary want.

When staying safe and pleasing your people become your primary wants, wanting is less risky. You don't have to ask and wait for answers. You can depend on yourself to do what it takes to keep things safe and to get the approval you need. Wanting things for yourself from inside yourself becomes too dangerous to know about. It will get you in trouble.

A strange small event that happened when I was ten or eleven made this very clear to me. We were staying at my father's parents' house in Iowa, and my parents did something unusual. They left the kids, four of us then, with our grandparents for a couple of hours one afternoon and went downtown to do some shopping. I didn't know what they were shopping for, but when they came back there were surprises – new pyjamas for each of the three little kids! My father handed them around. I waited for my turn, but there was nothing for me. I didn't say anything, but something showed on my face. My father was watching me. He said, "You shouldn't just want to get things."

I felt the shame of my wanting, and then he reached into a bag and handed me a package of pyjamas. I had to pretend to like them, but I didn't want them anymore.

Why did my father need to teach me that to want was shameful? Staying in his parents' house could have strange effects on him; maybe he was passing on to me something he had learned from them. Pondering on it now, I see that both of my parents were quite good at not wanting from inside themselves, and that this was a kind of virtue for them. "Trust and obey" tames all random, unruly want. Grabby Pup learns not to grab because he learns not to *want*. If one is Christ-like, one says, "Not my will, but Thine be done." Not very safe in themselves, my parents traded their personal, visceral wanting for wanting safety and approval instead – from the biggest father of them all, one who does not, it seems, condone anyone's just wanting to get things.

Shame keeps you inside the lines of wanting things safely, which means wanting what you've been given or will be given. As things get split into rights and wrongs, the part of you that wants more than you're given becomes not just troublesome but wrong. And we're not even talking about *desire* yet.

Even saying the word *desire* is a problem. That's because it has a *sexual* sound to it, which is also a word that's not to be spoken unless absolutely necessary. My mother had no time to vet my library books, and she believed in my reading, but when I brought home a stack of adult novels, she asked, "You're not reading anything *sexual* in those books, are you?" She said the word quickly, slurring it a bit, but clearly the question had to be asked of a twelve-year-old.

I said no, a lie of course, and she probably knew it. But her duty was done, like the duty of explaining how babies are made, part of the lecture on what to expect when you get your period. It was all functional, nothing to smile about, and the unspoken ambient feeling ran to distaste and disgust, not to desire or pleasure. Maybe it was just distasteful to have to talk to me about it. Because it's also true, and I think I knew it then, that my parents did desire each other and took pleasure in their sexual connection. But it seemed this desire and pleasure needed to be kept secret, hidden behind a curtain of shame.

Maybe we children needed not to know that there's pleasure in being sexual, because if we knew it, we'd desire it, which would lead directly to the sin of being sexual before we were supposed to be, which would be when we were married. Our bodily desires would be our undoing unless we were exceptionally self-disciplined; therefore, it was best not to encourage desire in any way. That's why masturbation would be dangerous. Ours was not a tradition that made sexual thoughts and self-experiments mortal sins; however, there were warnings about touching yourself down there. Of course, we children touched ourselves anyway and discovered ... Oh! Pleasure! Which was then our secret, not unlike the secrets we knew they kept.

There were secrets behind my mother's infamous, zany injunction, "You should always wash your hands in the morning because you never know where they've been at night."

I wonder whether she and my father kept their sexual desires and pleasures secret from themselves. Not that they wouldn't act on them again and again, once they were in the free space of being married. Ours was not a tradition in which conjugal sex was only for the purpose of procreation. Married adults could do what they liked, but they weren't supposed to amplify desire or revel in pleasure. On the contrary (as I imagine it), they took their pleasure while looking the other way, believing God was looking the other way, too.

It's not that God was against sex; after all, He created both the function of sex and the desire that made it happen. The pleasure part had slipped in rather by accident. But as long as people stayed within the rules and kept it quiet, He wouldn't mind their pleasure. They could keep it their secret. This was the vague story that made sense to me, and as I think of it now, I can see that this image of God is hardly a force roaring from Sinai, "Thou shalt not!" In this image, God is a bearded Victorian, dour and just a bit prissy, covering the legs of pianos.

All that to say, the problem wasn't sex. Victoria had her Albert. Despite their conflicts, my parents got around to sex quite often it seems, maybe even wordlessly treasuring their place of secret enjoyment. I was not told, in word or deed, that there was shame in being a sexual person. The shame was in enjoying being a sexual person, in desiring the pleasure of sex, in wanting something for yourself in such an explicitly embodied way. The deep suspicion of wanting, of desire for pleasure in general, drew sexuality into its ready-made swamp. (There is some truth in the old joke, "Why don't good Christians have sex standing up?" "Because it might lead to dancing.")

The shaming of desire means that by the time sexuality turns up, the damage is already done. As babies and young children, we are not driven by sexual desire; we are driven by a desire for relatedness with our nearby humans. We want the warm softness of ventral vagal safety: faces, hearts, and bellies open to connection. We desire sensual soothing and gentle, tender touch. We desire being loved openly and having our love received in return, with hugs, strokes, cheek-kisses, hands held. In the world I describe and knew, shame is the enemy of all such sensual desire, and not because it's sexual, but rather because it's a pleasurable something that we want. As with sex, the shame is in the desire itself, in the wanting. To dance is to linger in the wanting.

These are the physical correlatives of the emotional closeness we are driven by our human nature to desire. We want our emotions taken in with understanding and given back to us with care and emotional resonance. We want to see delight in the eyes looking at us, feel the energy of sharing intentions, thoughts, and vitality. We want engaged interest that will hold our mind in mind, our personhood in heart. We want to be seen and heard and talked with. We want emotional warmth, softness, openness. The intensity of this desire is as shameful as wanting physical connection, and for the same reason: just because we want it so much. The more we want it and don't get it, the more shameful the wanting becomes.

If we carry this shamed wanting through childhood and into adolescence it will get tangled up with sex one way or another, maybe as shameful discomfort with our bodies, maybe as compulsive "shameless" sex to get the closeness we're so hungry for. But inasmuch as the problem isn't sex, it won't be solved by sex. Sex won't teach us how to soften our shame-defences, our protection against vulnerable wanting, in order to be sensually and emotionally present. We need some capacity for safe, relaxed connection before our sexual desires can give us the pleasure we seek. The shame that shuts down our early deep wants and desires will block us later from realizing the potential of our sexuality.

When I say that relationship, not sex, is the first passionate, primal desire of human beings, I'm in good company. My first heroes of psychoanalytic theory – Ronald Fairbairn, Harry Guntrip, and Donald Winnicott – broke with the Freudian doctrine that the instinctual drives of sex and aggression are the motivating forces of the human psyche, the essence of our being. These members of the British Independent Group, along with others, taught that from early infancy onward, humans are fundamentally relationship-seeking beings.

This changes everything. Instead of neurosis or illness being a matter of an unconscious stand-off between unrecognized drive forces (id) and a clamp-down against them (superego), it's a matter of things having gone wrong in early relationships, and the wrong being carried forward as unconscious internal images of self-with-other that are distressing and destabilizing. The goal of treatment is not, then, to bring the forces of id and superego into consciousness so that the patient's ego can take control; the goal is to bring into consciousness the painful early relationships that patients keep repeating in life so they can eventually move on to finding safe, rewarding connections instead.

Analysts of the Independent Group were interested in their patients' earliest experiences of their parents, and like their Freudian colleagues, they hoped to help their patients find insight about psychic dynamics that were formed in childhood. But they didn't expect their patients to find repressed childhood sexual desire toward one parent and aggression toward the other. They expected them to find, instead, a wide variety of infantile strivings for connection met by many kinds of parental failure, leading to infantile states of terror, rage, numbness, isolation, and despair. (And someday, after this level of trauma was resolved, there might be later-childhood Oedipal issues for these patients to address.)

Transference, the psychoanalytic engine of change, took on a different character with the Independents. It was still a prime way for the unconscious to become conscious in the treatment relationship, but the patient's projections didn't take recognizable forms like sexual attraction or aggressive competition. Instead, the patient's experience of the analyst filled up with intense, preverbal relational feelings, the needy, desperate longings and the shamed, fearful hatreds of their infancy and earliest childhood.

Therefore, the analyst's job description shifted significantly. A patient's transference of such formless emotional intensity onto the analyst could not simply be noticed, understood, and interpreted. This intensity had to be held until it took some shape and meaning, which sometimes became clear only in the analyst's countertransference, or feelings about the patient's feelings. Members of the Independent Group began to believe that even when they could not put words to what was happening in the therapeutic relationship, they could be fully present in it, meeting, containing, and calming the intense emotion of their patients' regressed states. They believed that their nurturing kind of understanding would in itself be healing for their patients, a bridge toward healthy relationships beyond analysis.

Or to put it another way, the Independents accepted the fact that since the problem was essentially relational, and since the therapy was essentially a relational endeavour of talking and listening, the real relationship embedded in the therapy – the care and human connection that the analyst provides and the patient receives – could be made part of the treatment. This would be an inexact science, however, since from the patient's perspective at least, the "real relationship" or the "therapeutic alliance" would always be entangled with the primal projections this offer of connection would arouse.

In a best-case scenario, a sturdy real relationship or working alliance, developed in the therapy room and held in mind by both analyst and patient, would form a secure container for whatever welter of primal affect might emerge. Eventually the patient would have both the experience of intellectual and emotional insight into their own earliest, deepest dynamics and the experience of being joined with compassionate care while undergoing the tumultuous process of analysis. It would matter a great deal to their healing that they had been understood by this person, their analyst, and that they had experienced a deep, real connection with him or her.

But even in a best-case scenario, it could be a bumpy ride for both patient and analyst to get to that desired outcome. That's because a patient's regression into intense young feeling-states can take on a life of its own, temporarily (but for long stretches of time) obliterating their sense of being in alliance with their analyst, working collaboratively toward insight and healing. Instead, a patient may be overwhelmed with longing for their analyst's love, seeking and demanding proof of genuine care, or flooded by shame, rage, and despair, experiencing their analyst as indifferent or rejecting. This constant upsurge of turbulent, primitive interpersonal emotion can become for a time a patient's only reality in therapy, so intense that it threatens the stability of the therapeutic alliance.

Why would I be reading this theory at thirty when I had no intention of being in psychoanalysis or becoming a psychoanalyst? First, I did intend to become a psychotherapist, and I found that the insight-oriented therapy that interested me called itself "psychodynamic." Psychodynamic therapy turned out to be the basics of psychoanalytic theory applied to a less intense form of practice – face-to-face conversations instead of using a couch, and weekly sessions instead of several sessions each week. Second, I had an urgent need to understand what was happening to me in my weekly psychodynamic therapy.

I had quit my Ph.D. program, fallen apart, and found a therapist who helped me recover and re-orient to becoming a social worker therapist and being the mom of three small children. I ended that first therapy, but now I knew myself well enough to recognize that I was still anxious and depressed. In hopes of feeling better, I decided to go back to therapy. The therapist I chose was a woman old enough to be my mother; coincidentally, my mother and she had the same first name. As far as I knew, I chose her because she worked in the office next to the therapist who had seen me through the crisis, and I knew he looked up to her as a mentor.

I don't remember my first session with her. I do remember coming out of an evening university class, one of my MSW prerequisites, and thinking about the session. I stopped until the hall cleared and I was alone. The hall was long with a staircase at the end, and in my memory, dimly lit. I was seized by a need to decide something. *If you go ahead with this therapy, you are going to feel a LOT toward this woman. Then what will happen? Do you want this?*

I had no idea what would happen, but I realized I had already decided. I did want this, but I needed to own it. *Are you all in then? Are you going to go for it?* I stood there with a *yes* in my mind, though I knew

I didn't know what it meant. Then I walked down the steps toward my bike and the trip home.

I said yes to desire that felt neither sexual nor sensual. As the weeks and months passed, the desire became an obsession with the time I spent in this therapist's presence, seeking her warm, quick understanding, the feeling that I was interesting to her. I desperately wanted her to enjoy me, respond to me, hear me, see me. I replayed our conversation as I walked for an hour after a session; I wrote pages in my journal of things I could have said to her, things I might say next time. If she mentioned a book she had read, I would read it. When she told me about her plan to attend a professional conference, I signed up, as a student therapist, for the conference.

My obsession felt secret and safe, but it was not pleasurable. My desire to be special to her, deeply connected to her, was as huge as my whole internal world, but I knew I'd only ever be a small part of her working week, not ever part of her real life. She couldn't truly care for me; I would never really matter. This bitterness would well up in me if she failed to understand me or felt distant, and then it would spill over as resentment. She would be patient but not pleased. I felt trapped by something I couldn't control. That's when I began to read theory to try to find out what was happening to me.

The concept of transference was waiting for me on page one. What a relief to read that these feelings that stirred so much desire and shame in me were totally expectable! But transference took on different shades of meaning in different kinds of psychodynamic theory. I chose the theory that made the best sense of my feelings – they weren't sexual longings, but longings to be understood, beloved, and treasured, mixed with the despair of knowing this could never happen. It made sense to me that these feelings were transferred to my therapist from my relationships with my parents.

I brought my therapist a dream: *I'm standing in front of a closed door. Its glass pane is frosted, opaque. I open the door, and you're sitting at the far end of a long table. The room is a small, bare classroom with no windows. I have to sit at the near end of the long table and explain myself to you. I can't see your eyes behind your glasses.* When I told my therapist the dream, she was pleased that I knew it was about my mother. But interpreting the transference didn't change the feelings.

So I read more. I read about people locked into a split transference, on the one side desperately wanting to be a good self with a good mother, on the other side desperately trying to escape being a bad self with a bad mother. The hopeless, intense pain of their cyclical struggle made sense to me. I read that the only way out was to grow up out of that split state, so fraught and all-consuming but in the end just a childish fantasy. I dreamed of two jetliners flying side by side until their paths split, and then one blew up, killing all on board. I decided I needed to grow up out of the intensity of my transference.

I told my therapist about my reading, the dream, and my decision. She told me she admired my capacity to do the work. Looking back across four decades, it seems we ended not long after, though I'm sure there was a winding down process. Did I grow up out of my desire to be so intensely connected? Even now I'd like to say yes, but the truth is no. I found a theoretically sophisticated box of shame for my desire so that I could put it away with a gesture of competent maturity.

Here I am outing myself as one of those clients whom therapists find challenging because they want too much from us, with too much intensity. They want to know what we think and feel, and too much rides on what we say. They want our approval, our love, our undivided attention, and they fall into silent shame at the slightest break between us. They hate our holidays and the fact that we have other clients, even while they also hate their childish "dependency" feelings.

I have often wondered, thinking about myself and all such intensely desiring clients, why some people never have to do the work of therapy by way of messy transference, and other people just can't help themselves. If they go into therapy, that's what happens. They start wanting what they can't have and suffer on account of their desire. It's a mystery, I've thought. Unfortunately, some of us are just wired that way.

But now I'm thinking it's no mystery. Those of us who suffer in transference have been suffering the shame of our desire to love and to be loved since before we can remember. The intensity of our shame matches the intensity of our want denied, a dissociated suffering that long predates entering therapy. The want denied wakes up in the presence of a therapist who is kind, warm, and inviting, where there is no agenda for therapy but to feel what you feel, talk about it, and be understood.

The want comes back full force, but since it's already want *denied*, shame comes with it full force. When our shame is too much to bear, we make the therapist the embodiment of what shames us, the embodiment of all we want that must be denied. Then we can feel hurt and rageful at someone instead of feeling the intensity of our own shame. Or we can pick a lesser shame; we can pack up our hurt and rage as pathology, and move on. That's what I did. But it didn't last.

It didn't last because as soon as I finished my social work degree, I went on to learn to be a therapist. I found myself in a program of experiential training that gave me just what I needed to learn as a person as well as what I needed to learn to become a client-centred psychodynamic therapist. I did six hours of training a week, all of it in groups, and almost all the groups were process oriented. That meant I had to listen and speak from my heart. I had to feel my emotions, ask to be understood, dare to be in conflict, have and communicate empathy for my peers' histories, fears, and desires. Groups activated my family of origin dynamics and lit up issues that needed work.

Being in therapy was a requirement of the program. It was suggested that I see someone who would help me be not so much in my head, not so worried about doing things right. Asking around, I became intrigued by a therapist I had never met. I'd heard, however, that he had come from my religious tradition but had turned into something of a rebel and outcast. He was on my institute's informal "approved" list because he had once been a student there and was fundamentally psychodynamic. But then he had gone on to learn various kinds of emotionally expressive therapies – from Gestalt to expressive arts to bioenergetics. I figured it would be hard for me to be too much for him.

But would I want too much from him? Yes, I would, and this time the intensity of my transference feelings didn't surprise me. His welcome surprised me. He didn't pretend that he could satisfy my primitive longings to be simply held and loved, but he encouraged me to be inside the want with him, to feel how it came from a healthy place a long time ago. His ease quieted my shame, and my desire became warmth in my body. He met me with matching warmth and softness.

He welcomed the other side, too, my rage and despair about what I had missed and would never have. He said maybe my anger was as big as the huge red bolster in the corner of the room, the one people could punch and whack if they wanted to. I didn't want to. He said, "It's true, you can't go ever go back in time. And this is only one hour a week. But every time you come, take all you can!"

I took all I could of his permission to say whatever I felt, including, for several weeks, my childish protest about a long holiday he was planning to take to Europe. One day he sat up straight and told me firmly, "Well, I'm going." Then I was a child who had hit a limit, and I brought my reparation the next week: a tiny card I had made for him. He smiled and thanked me, and then he pulled out his wallet and tucked the card inside it. "See," he said, "You'll be right here with me the whole time I'm away." What he said felt real to me, and it told me that my desire to be always held in his mind did not need to be shamed or forgiven.

He was a master of Winnicott's transitional space, the space where things are neither true nor false, but simply real.[1] Here playing is reality. I played in that space as hard as I had ever played basketball, and it called out the embodied emotion my right brain had been holding on its own for so long. Emotion emerged in tears and anger, but also in visual images and body feelings, in dreamscapes and little-kid stories enacted, in simple improvised psychodramas about being lost and found, alone and together. Emotional meanings became word meanings as we sat and talked, and I traced out the patterns and connections of my inner life.

I began to write him letters, sometimes weekly, that spelled out the meanings that were coming to me. He welcomed my letters kindly and understood that I didn't need to talk about them. It was enough for me – it was exactly right – that he read them. As I had written them, he had already been the perfect reader in my mind. I had told my story before, but now it belonged to a self I could feel from the inside out. As he heard me, read me, and felt with me, I felt held in his emotional self – in his right brain, I would say now, though I didn't know to say that then.

I understand now that this is why this therapy worked so well for me: it was all about right-brain to right-brain connectedness. His consistent soft, warm ventral vagal presence made it safe for me to search for this nonverbal connected state and then, within it, to be whoever I was that day. I also understand now that the various expressive modalities he offered were sometimes the vehicles for our work, but they were never the essence of it. I believe his presence and his capacity to connect emotional-self-to-emotional-self would have been enough. I must have believed that then, because I never decided to train in any of those modalities; instead, I remained a talk therapist and honed my capacities for presence and emotional connection.

It took more than three years (not long by psychoanalytic standards), but there came a time when I had wanted, suffered, and grieved enough, when I had been found, held, and understood well enough. I dreamed that I went to my therapist's funeral, and then when I looked into the casket, he wasn't in there; my mother was. I said to my dreamer-self, "Okay, enough already. I get it." At the end of the road of a regressive therapy, there is always a funeral.

I felt my emotional self moving toward an ending that was not just loss. This space had been a good place to be a child, but now I wanted to grow up, and I needed something different, a new kind of beginning. I told my therapist, "I think I need to be with a strong woman therapist for a while. Strong older women scare me, but I think I need someone to help me get over the fear, someone I could want to be like 'when I grow up.' You know?" He did know, and he had an older colleague in mind. He made the referral and wished me well on my new adventure.

She was scary. She was one of the battleships – so named by my philosopher friend Henk, wary of them for his own reasons. He had noticed these middle-aged women in the hallways of the therapy centre he now visited weekly. They intended to be noticed. They moved and spoke as if they were entitled to respect. They took up space. Some of that, I now understand, was social privilege. They came from affluence; they were North Toronto women. Their mothers had been matrons, but they weren't. Nor were they matriarchs. They were second-wave white feminists, Jewish and Christian, consciously resisting the patriarchy in which they were embedded as the wives or ex-wives of doctors, accountants, and businessmen.

They owned their own offices; they were making their own livings, pursuing excellence in their profession at conferences and in study groups. Several had been family physicians before becoming psychotherapists. They had all been trained at the institute where I had been trained, but a generation earlier, when lay psychotherapy was brand-new in Toronto, and women making a profession of it was extraordinary. Grateful to have been part of this ground-breaking training program, many of them gave back by volunteering an hour a week to supervise one of the institute's students. Two of them had been supervisors for me when I was in training.

I was now half-time in private practice myself, and half-time a director of training at this institute, recognized for my leadership skills and my capacity to link theory with practice. I was fully aware of the weird juxtaposition of my feeling small and my stepping into this role and doing it well. I had always been a parentified child, doing much more than I should have, given my dearth of inner resources. At least now I felt settled and coherent in my core self, I recognized the parentified-child problem, and I thought maybe something could be done about it. Women with power scared me, but I had to know: How do you do woman and power at the same time?

I wanted to grow up internally, sheltered by a woman wiser and stronger than I was, someone who would be on my side and could show me how to be wise and strong myself. I simply felt that this could happen in therapy, but I was also backed up by the new self psychology theory I was reading. What I loved most about self psychology was how it could embrace the self-needs expressed in transference and hold them in a sustained empathy that created space for them to grow into self-strength. Later I saw the larger picture: as a system developed to help narcissistically injured patients (chronically shamed patients), self psychology could not, by definition, participate in the shaming of "immature" needs or in the shaming of anyone's desire to have them met.

In self psychological terms, my desire was this: I wanted to idealize a powerful woman. Theory told me it would be a positive transference, not one to suffer with or to have to renounce, but one that over time could become a positive part of my self-structure, filling in something that was missing. Theory also told me that there would likely be some negative transference that would repeat themes from my past, but that this could be worked through and resolved in order to get back to the positive. So I was prepared to throw myself into a therapy relationship once again and feel whatever I was going to feel.

My particular battleship was not a total stranger to me. In my institute role, I had filed supervision reports that came in from her. I had welcomed her into a large group meeting before she sat in as support to her supervisee in a case conference. I knew that she had learned and taught bioenergetics for a while, but had moved on from that to self psychology and Stone Center theory. I think I also knew that she was married with grown children, maybe even grandchildren. Things get known in communities. I suppose she also knew some general things about me before we finally met as client and therapist.

I remember our first meeting – or a collage of similar meetings. She welcomed me graciously with a nod toward where I was supposed to sit, a cane-back rocking chair opposite her matching chair. The room was tastefully decorated: textured light peach wallpaper, framed prints in blues and greys, a thick wool accent rug, glass shelving with books and objects interspersed, a potted ficus near the window, a small vase of flowers on the long, narrow glass table that ran beside our two rockers.

Sitting easily and solidly in her chair, she said, "Tell me about yourself, why you're here." She listened with both feet on the ground, arms on the rocker arms, fingertips steepled together and toward me. Sometimes she raised the steeple to her chin for a while. She was easy to talk to, a friendly face with warm eyes when she smiled, and all the while I talked, I was taking in whatever I could learn about who she was.

Late fall when we started, she wore soft but formal pantsuits made of a thick jersey, similar outfits in various colours, and always with soft leather slip-on shoes. When spring and summer came, she wore roomy shirts and cotton slacks with Birkenstocks. She didn't bother with make-up, and her hair was wavy and greying naturally, cut in an easy brush-back style. So far so good. I didn't wear dresses or make-up either; I wouldn't have to aspire to a version of woman alien to me. My therapist had made a good referral.

I'm sure I talked about the things in my life that troubled me, but I don't remember what they were. I talked as a way to immerse myself in the relationship, and I found that as we got to know each other, the connectedness I had learned to seek was possible between us. I knew I was trying to engage the heart and mind of my "new mom" and I loved feeling her response as she shared her empathy and emotional energy with me.

And then one day I walked in and she was the enemy. I sat down but I couldn't look at her. What was happening? She waited, perplexed. I was quiet until it came to me. "I think this is about my mother," I told her. "There's a place in me where I believe she hates me, like she would destroy me if she could." Why would my psyche be throwing up this projection at this moment in this space? It didn't matter. I just had to get through it. "So I'm feeling like you hate me," I said, standing up and backing away, full of an old fear.

"Well, that might be your mother," she said. "I don't know. But it's not me!" She was standing now, too, beside her chair. "Look at me. See me." I looked at her. "I'm the same me as I was last week and I will be next week!" Her indignant certainty broke the spell. No, she was not my mother. I could send that psychodrama away with a nod to my British Independent mentors. Yes, the Oedipal stuff may come up later – and it doesn't have to be a big deal.

But there was another eruption of indignation from her later, baffling at the time, but now I'm thinking of it as a bookend to the first – the developmental way through the feelings of competition that can confound any mother-daughter (or father-son) relationship. If those feelings are real, you can't just ignore them. They aren't the end of the world; nobody has to die. But something has to happen for them to take their rightful place. Here's what happened to us.

I started it. Sometimes on the glass table next to my therapist's chair there'd be a book of therapy theory she was reading, which could entice me into a conversational gambit. Theory was fun for me. This time I had already read the book and I had a strong opinion about it. As I was making my excellent point, I noticed that suddenly she was sitting forward, full of something she wanted to say. I stopped and waited for it. "You!" she said. "You ... are an *upstart!*"

I gazed at her, shocked at the heat in her voice, not sure if I should be hurt. Was she responding from defensive insecurity? Was this a fight? But she didn't seem angry, just full of herself, gamely ready to take me on. A strange bubble of joy rose up in me and I blurted out a laugh, palms up, like, "Yes, that's me; what can I do?" She smiled back briefly and relaxed, seeming to shake off some surprise at what had burst out of her. I would come to know that she trusted her instincts first and theory second. My reaction would have told her what was happening – that she didn't need to take her words back or apologize.

In that moment, I felt that I had been met by strength and taken down a peg, but without malice. It was clear that this really had nothing to do with her book or my thoughts on it. This was about my big energy. Her reaction to it was disconcerting, maybe to both of us, and my response to it all stranger still. Why would a knockdown draw from me bewildered relief and even joy, of all things? I had no idea. I just felt what I felt.

Thinking about it now, I'm certain that the Oedipal idea misses the gist of what happened here between my therapist and me. Maybe my mother and I had, indeed, competed for my father's love, and here was a repetition of that deadly competition, which I would – appropriately – lose. But this didn't feel like a win/lose interaction to me. Furthermore, there's so much about the play of power between a parent and child that has no third person involved. A child needs to know: Can you let me be powerful, challenge you hard, and also not let me defeat you?

Self psychology asks: What kind of response to that crucial question does a growing self need? An optimal response from a parent will have two parts, well balanced: first, "Bring it on; I like it," and second, "I'm here in my own power. You can take me on, but you can't wipe me out." An insecure parent won't meet the challenge, which leaves a child ashamed of wanting to be big and strong. But the child might push through anyway and end up all alone with an unsupported, precarious "bigness," also an occasion for shame.

I had been taught to be ashamed of having large, strong energy. But I had pushed through anyway, and now I felt alone with the ungrounded fragility of my "bigness." Being called an upstart knocked me down to size. But I didn't feel attacked; instead, I felt my therapist's embodied willingness to be her own kind of strong and take me on. Because she was unafraid to meet my energy and tussle with it, I would have a chance to grow into real, supported power instead of fake, upstart power. I think that's why I felt joy.

I doubt my therapist knew why she blurted out that word "upstart." She sensed something between us and did something about it. My response was just as unthought, seizing on something I needed, whatever her intention. But what we enacted brought the push and pull of power between us to more conscious awareness, if still unspoken. It settled something just before we were yanked into the real world together.

The group with whom my therapist shared a teaching practice and an office building asked her to ask me whether I would consider becoming a partner in their group. With misgivings, she passed on the question. It was late winter; we had been working together for just over a year. If I said yes, we would have to end therapy in the summer to start as colleagues in the fall.

Years later she told me that she had always regretted asking me. It wasn't fair. Given what I was working on with her, how could I have said no?

I did try to consider both sides. I talked with an accountant, my husband, my peers. The accountant was so-so, the others were encouraging. This was a group of highly respected senior therapists. How could joining them not help the trajectory of my career?

For me it was simple in the end. If what I wanted was to grow up unafraid in the presence of a strong woman, well, I had already done a good chunk of that work. And how much more satisfying would it be to finish the work in the real world as a real colleague, not in the pretend world of therapy! I actually knew that I couldn't say no. Did that mean I *should* say no? The question gave me pause, but in the end I didn't think so.

When I told her yes, she asked me if I was sure. Then we talked about ending before her long August holiday. It felt sad but manageable under the circumstances, and still far away. A week or two later, there was a new development. She had been on a list for hip replacement months into the future. Suddenly a cancellation spot was offered to her for April 5, and she took it. She would be away for two months. I was as devastated and bereft as a kid without her mom. Sick and tired of living the intensities of my therapy life alone and in secret, I told some people close to me why I was sad. Talking helped. When she came back, I felt ready for the next goodbye.

I believed I was good at ending my therapies, having had some practice at it. I knew the cost, but I could grieve my losses at the end of the road, come out of my transference states, and move on. In our last session in July, she told me she was closing my file, and that she had something for me. I had, of course, written her letters that I hadn't needed to talk about. She had received them graciously. For this occasion, she had put them into a binder, and now she was giving them back to me. As a marker of what was happening, this felt exactly right. We didn't say, "See you in September." That would be something else.

In September, I moved my practice into the building and became a new member of an established system. We were a group of four men and three women. Weekly staff meetings included lunch and personal sharing time. I was introduced to their model of training. A class was about to graduate, and we talked about starting up a new class the next fall. They wanted to hear my ideas about texts that would help synthesize developmental and intersubjectivity theory. I saw why I had been brought on board – they needed my capacities to create curriculum and teach theory – but I didn't mind. They were competent adults in their own right; it was a fair deal. I wasn't being parentified. I saw that they were just ordinary people with their faults and failings. I didn't mind that either. I wanted to be with older adults who could be frank about the journey of life, open about troubled times and difficult feelings.

Later that first year, my former-therapist-now-colleague and I decided that we would offer a short-term women's group. We met in my office, a mid-afternoon tea time, to plan our approach and advertising. The group turned out to be small and not a complete success. She and I didn't yet have an intuitive sense of how to play off each other as leaders. I realized that I hardly knew her as a person, so I suggested we have more tea-time talks. She knew so much about me, not that we talked about what she knew, now inside a closed file. I wanted to get to know her, I said. Would she tell me about herself?

She was happy to talk, and it was not all one-way. Those were lovely weeks, months, of becoming friends over tea. We discovered we had both been camp counsellors, canoe trippers, "sports" in our youth. Her mother had been dismayed about her tomboy ways, but she had been a father's daughter anyway. She had loved having babies, then children, and her three were now so much older than my three. It was wonderful to hold a grandchild, she said. I went camping with my kids; she went with her family to the cottage her father had built. This was easy sharing, no surprises.

I also learned she had grown up Baptist and had come to therapy by way of encounter groups sponsored by her Anglican diocese. She didn't go to church now, but she was in a women's spirituality group and read feminist theology. I hadn't expected that. She lent me a book on women's friendship, and I took to heart the parts she had highlighted.

As we came closer to matters of the heart, she began to share some of the troubles in her life, a deep loss and sadness in her family, and before that, a radical break in her relationship with her husband. She thought she could forgive him. They were reconciling for the sake of the family and their long history together. I was touched by her openness, glad she trusted me, relieved and grateful to be moving further with her toward being women in the world together, both of us vulnerable and strong.

One day when tea time ended, I was walking her to the door as always. But then we stopped and looked at each other. Who knows why the not-knowing suddenly falls away, how the truth becomes available? We still had a chance to turn away from it, but now it would be a choice. We chose, instead, to move into the truth of the moment.

I had never kissed a woman before, nor had she, but it felt absolutely right. Exquisite. Breathtaking. Astonishing. All such language for what words can't say, but if you've ever fallen in love, you know. Then imagine that you've been alive for nearly forty years, or for more than sixty years, and you've never felt that feeling before, not even close. Imagine having spent years in therapy learning how to be emotionally open, physically present, soft, warm, available, and then suddenly your sexual being arrives in that place. Imagine that this arriving means coming into a space of desire so profoundly forbidden that you could never even dream of it.

I was not ashamed to come into my desire. I was exultant: *Hallelujah!* in my body and soul. There would be plenty of shaming trouble to come, and the tricky work of trying to make a good-faith space for my desire in the world, but I was never ashamed of having fallen blissfully, jubilantly in love. Nor was she ever ashamed of her desire and how she went for it.

Eventually we would have many years together, my battleship partner and I. Almost a year ago now, during Mary's time of dying, her daughter Madeleine said to me, "You have been the love of her life, you know." Yes, this I know for sure, and it comforts me.

If this were an autobiography, I would now have to write about the shaming trouble that was to come, having just foreshadowed it. But this is a series of essays, and right now I'm writing about shame and desire. The shaming trouble will come back around in the next essay, which will have the uninviting title, *Shame and Being Right or Wrong*. It can wait.

I want to write about a kind of shamed desire that can get lost in the shuffle around sexuality when it's understood as sexual orientation. The orientation questions are relational: To whom are you attracted? What arouses your desire for another? With whom will you fall in love?

Let me note, parenthetically, that these are sometimes called questions of sexual preference, as if we have a range of choices and we get to pick the one we like the best. As if we could make do fine with a second choice, or a third. "I prefer apples, but I'll have an orange if that's all you've got. Or a kiwi." I wonder if there's anyone whose sexual desire runs outside the normative average who would be pleased to call their desire their preference. It seems to me a mealy-mouthed word that slips a little blame and shame in sideways, denying the visceral reality of desire, the fact that we do not choose this. For the record, loving a woman is not something I "prefer." This is not even what I choose. My desire is who I am.

But I want to write about another kind of desire around sexuality and identity, one just as vulnerable to shame. I mean the lively, visceral want in each of us to step out into the world as an attractive, desirable, gendered human being; our wanting to be an embodied self with confidence, pleasure, and pride – no matter what the most genuine expression of our gender identity might be, and no matter how that lines up with the gender we were assigned at birth. Many trans people walk heads-up toward the possibility of physical and psychological violence, all of it shaming, because they know and say with pleasure and pride, "This is who I am."

I won't speak for them; I will speak for myself and maybe for others who are not transgender, but who also don't live assigned genders according to expectations. I want to say that this, too, is not a choice; it's an identity. It's independent of sexual orientation. It can be source of shame, externally and internally, all on its own. I'm grateful for this strange grace that came to me by way of coming out: I was given space to be a "different kind of woman" and thus given a chance finally to step up to this gender-shame and face it down bit by bit. This is not a small thing.

I believe that if I were a man, I would know it by now, and I would transition in one way or another to become a man in the world. I am very fortunate to live in a decade and city in which that choice would be relatively safe, and that the choice would be honoured and even celebrated within my immediate family and community. But much as you might think otherwise to look at me sometimes, I don't feel that I am a man. I am a manly kind of woman, and that's a woman – if we have to come back to the binary, either man or woman. It seems the world asks that of us. (But how many genders, how many versions of non-binary, might there be if we didn't have to do that?)

You may have noticed that I don't call myself lesbian. It's a fine word, but although it might be technically accurate about my sexual orientation, it's wrong about my gender. Speaking gender, I'm not a lesbian; I'm a butch dyke. It's a dying breed, some say; more and more butches will transition out. I imagine, however, that a certain percentage of birth-assigned girls will keep on being born to the breed and then, with or without support, start growing up in a butch dyke direction. I'd like to tell them,

> Hey, you can be a boy if that's who you are and what you want, but it's also totally ok to be a boy kind of girl. You can wear what you like, walk how you like, get your hair cut short, play baseball all day. It's kinda fun to be a boy kind of girl. Some of us are just born that way.

It's kinda fun to be a manly kind of woman, now that I'm getting clear of the shame of it. I can smile kindly to put at ease all those strangers who misgender me and then realize their mistake. I can shop insouciantly in men's departments. And in women's departments for those crossover items that keep 'em guessing. I don't mind being told I'm "hot" in a tux or suit.

But my favourite pants are jeans, with either boots or Birkenstocks. The latter often with socks, I'm sorry. The shirts matter: button up and button down; stripes, plaid, plain. Inside the shirts? I wear a bra. Supportive and comfortable, rather flattening, not that it matters. I'm ok to keep my breasts. "Imagine that being a choice," I say to my eleven-year-old self who felt sick about those nubs of nipples in the mirror. "There is something we could do about it." But it turns out I don't want to.

I like my breasts because they hold for me body-memories of the soft, warm pleasure of breastfeeding my children, daytimes rocking and nighttimes lying close. I like my breasts because they can bring pleasure to me and to a woman who loves breasts as much as I do. Female genitalia? Also kinda nice.

The dour Victorian imposter-god who haunted my childhood is raising his eyebrows at me. I tell him I've seen the legs of pianos too; don't be so prissy, and he disappears. I call up the idea of the power of love in the universe. "And where would you be without the power of female genitalia? And breasts?" I hear a chuckle. It's just me, but I'm not alone.

Mary liked to tell my friends that she taught me how to play. If she said so in my hearing, I would just smile; it was true. She didn't mean golf, though that was also true. I see her gazing down the fairway after a mighty swing and a long drive, one hand in her pocket, the other on her club. "The one that brings you back," she says with a grin. Then it's my turn to step up to the tee, the shot perfect in my mind until it's happened. She did adore playing that game well, and she loved to have me with her on the course, learning to enjoy whatever happened.

What Mary taught me is that life doesn't have to be just work. That's what she was telling my friends – that she helped me learn an attitude of play. Life is for finding pleasure and reaching for what you want. Love your work and your hobbies, your friends and family, love your gardens, flowers, music, and books, love your dog. She was rarely idle, but she was rarely doing something she didn't want to do.

Desire is trustworthy and nothing to be ashamed of. Follow your desire. Mary never had to say that out loud or even silently to herself; she just knew it in her bones.

She hung on in palliative care long after she had stopped eating not because she was afraid to die but because she didn't want to leave the party. She wasn't in pain. As long as Mary could see me, hold my hand, and listen to her music, there was pleasure for her. As long as she could still enjoy something and love somebody, she wanted to be here. The dementia seemed to fade with fasting. One day she said to me, her eyes and her voice clear, "I want to stay." But then came the day when she was too tired to speak or open her eyes or squeeze my hand. I played her music anyway, believing she could hear, and I told her, as I did every night, that I loved her. In the early morning, she quietly slipped away.

I sat with her body, still warm to my hand but very thin and small and still, the hollows of her eyes and cheeks so deep. That memory intruded on my thoughts for months. Mary had warned me about this many years before, unintentionally. She had told me about her mother's long dying of cancer and how for months after she died, all she could remember of her mother's face was the death mask. This was frightening, but it passed. Eventually good memories of her mother came back to her, and in the end they mattered much more than the death memory.

I have been surprised at how much has come back to me, and how clearly, as I've been writing here. Since it seems I'm able to call up memories now, I'll ask for the one I want that will bring this essay to the ending it needs. I want to remember dancing.

I never learned to dance properly, but for a slow dance it didn't matter. It just sometimes happened at home, unplanned, when the right music was playing. One of us would find the other, our feet would cooperate, and our bodies would move to the music, belly to belly, heart to heart, cheek to cheek, warm and soft, lingering in desire.

You'd think that an early memory would be coming to me from a time when desire was new and fresh, but no, it's at the condo, maybe six years ago. From here I can see that Mary is failing a bit already. She's steady enough on her feet to dance without the cane, though. I think it's Christmas, and the music might be a TV special. We've had a good day, just the two of us, all our little rituals. I don't know who finds the other, but there we are, slow dancing in the space between the pantry and the living room. My memory must be taken by the delightful surprise of it. We might be sixty-four and eighty-eight, but we are suddenly slowly dancing, and desire moves between us. We smile at each other like, "Wow! Did you feel that? I did!"

Desire came to us once as a gift with the power to burst through a wall of shame. Now it's there as a quiet grace that has weathered trouble and strife. It will endure as tenderness right through to the end.

NOTE

1 Donald W. Winnicott, "Transitional Objects and Transitional Phenomena," in *Playing and Reality* (New York: Routledge, 1989), 1–25.

REFERENCE

Winnicott, Donald W. "Transitional Objects and Transitional Phenomena." In *Playing and Reality*, 1–25. New York: Routledge, 1989.

Essay Five

If chronic shame lurks in the shadows of your psyche to repeat *ad nauseam* that there's something wrong with you, one way to silence it is to be as right as you can possibly be. If needy vulnerability dwells within you as shameful badness, a cloak of highly competent goodness provides excellent cover. This had been my life strategy for managing chronic shame: to be seen as a capable, responsible person who could always be trusted to do the right thing. What I did about my accident of falling in love would flatten this persona.

I could say it was just as well. My criteria for making ethical choices had come from outside of me, from my family, communities, and religious tradition. It was high time for me to develop a more internal locus of responsibility and moral agency. But like all shame-prone people, I would remain painfully sensitive to being seen as wrong, and so this would be a gruelling marathon. I would be wrong in so many eyes for so many reasons. Or that's how I would feel.

That's how it is with shame. It's feeling totally wrong in the eyes of others. Thus the question of doing right or wrong becomes the question of *being* right or wrong. If I'm right, I'm accepted; if I'm wrong, I'm exiled. So says shame, its reality so stark and simple because it comes from a very young place in me, from a time when the eyes of my caregivers first turned angry and cold because of bad things I did.

By then my attachment relationships with them had been compromised by misattunement and anxiety, and so there were plenty of random bad feelings inside me to blend in with the bad I had done and saw reflected in their eyes, making me feel all bad. But I learned that I could feel better by being good and making their eyes smile at me again. It seems I got stuck there, in the place where the goodness of my being depended on the approval in their eyes.

Little kids don't have to get stuck there, but to move forward they need their caregivers to take the lead as mentors about the meanings

DOI: 10.4324/9781003499121-5

of good and bad, right and wrong. I needed my parents to allow me space for my differences, to talk to me about what I felt, and to explore ideas about what's fair or unjust, kind or cruel. By sharing simple versions of their own internal moral compass, they could have encouraged me to learn to make choices based on my wanting to be fair, kind, and good from the inside out.

My parents didn't do that kind of mentoring. Their moral compass always had an external reference. A favourite Sunday School song taught us to mind what we saw, heard, said, and did -- because our Father up above was always watching us. The song gave us no instruction about how we were supposed to behave. Just knowing that God's eyes were upon us would make us the right kind of careful.

I was led to believe that God has told us in His Word whatever we need to know about right and wrong. I have since learned that it's hard to find direction on specific moral issues in the Bible. I've also learned that group moralities determine how communities read scripture. People believe that what they see as right and wrong is what God sees and therefore what scripture says. There are so many eyes to be careful of in this shame-based system of moral rectitude!

If what's right is defined by something infallible outside of us, it wouldn't have been proper for my parents to teach me to choose right from wrong based on fallible conscience. They couldn't help me grow into the kind of moral agency one gets to by working through mistakes – because in a shame-based system, perfection may be unattainable, but it's always the goal. A right answer can be found for every ethical question. What's not right is wrong, or sin.

This system of external accountability is far from grounded in the everyday wrongs, hurts, and conflicts of life. But everyday messy relationship is the only place where children and adolescents can learn everyday moral reasoning and moral agency. I wish my parents had been able to let me be in conflict with them and assure me that my emotions and choices belonged to me. I wish they had been able to be honest about the conflict between them, so much in our faces but never acknowledged as a problem, and honest, too, about mistakes they made in their parenting.

I didn't need my parents to aspire to perfection and privately ask for God's forgiveness whenever they failed. I needed to see them trying to be responsible and kind, and then when they failed, trying to make things right with the people they had hurt. I needed to see them as moral agents making considered choices about their behaviours in the family and their ethical positions in the world. They could have taught me by example, but words would have helped, too.

Words might have helped me understand shame as an emotion I would feel when my behaviour had injured my relationship with others and with myself. I could have learned that if I said to others and to myself that I was sorry and that I would do better, the shame would ease. I could have been told that shame was supposed to be only as big as the disappointing thing I had done, and it was never supposed to be about all of me. I wish I had known that there would always be parts of me that I wasn't proud of, but that people could love me anyway, and help me manage those parts – because they had learned to manage the parts of themselves they weren't proud of.

Words could have helped with guilt, too. I don't believe that children can be protected from the realities of harm done in the world. They listen to the news and adult conversations; they see what happens on the street, in school, in their own homes. They know that sometimes they do things that hurt others. Like any perceptive child, I knew all this, and I needed someone to speak frankly with me about doing wrong and feeling guilty. I needed to know that guilt is what people should feel when they have done real harm for which they need to be accountable and make reparation. I needed to see adults taking responsibility for harms they had done. If I hurt someone myself, I needed help learning how to be accountable for my deed, as well as how to get to the other side of feeling ashamed.

I understand that these ways of being with me were not available to my parents. It's not that they chose to deprive me of a moral education. In fact, they believed that they were giving me the very best moral education in teaching me to be always aware of the eyes of God upon me. I'm writing this not to blame them for what they couldn't do; rather, to try to understand what kind of moral development I had come to in my late thirties and why my inner resources were limited as I faced a crucial ethical dilemma.

———————

I desperately wanted someone to tell me what I should do, someone wise and responsible who understood my new reality. I had assumed

I was heterosexual, I was married with children, and now I knew without a doubt that I was homosexual. I had fallen in love for the first time and realized that the love between my husband and me failed to do justice to either of us. The person I now loved had once, not very long ago, been my therapist. What was I supposed to do?

I could see myself through the eyes of people who would tell me exactly what I should do. My family's religious tradition believed that although I might not be able to stop being homosexual, acting on this state of being would be sin in the eyes of God. Furthermore, falling in love might happen to people, but acting on such lust to break the vows of marriage would be utterly wrong. My professional community was moving toward the position that a sexual relationship between persons who had once been therapist and client, no matter the length of the therapy or how it ended, was always an abuse of a therapist's power, a violation of a client's vulnerability.

I wanted so deeply not to be the person those eyes would see. But I couldn't undo the experience of having discovered something alive and beautiful in myself and for myself, something I hadn't known or thought possible. I wanted to honour and keep what I had found, even with all those eyes on me, even though I didn't know what that would mean. I wouldn't go back and put it all away. I couldn't. I would go forward, though I had no experience making decisions against the rules, decisions that could cause pain, that might be wrong.

I decided that if I were to let this be real, Nigel should be the first person to know, and so after the kids were in bed one evening, I asked to talk. He asked me if I would first read an open letter he'd just written, part of his work in a study group in our new congregation. The letter supported gay and lesbian rights in the church. I read it, offered my comments, and was grateful for an easy segue: "It's so strange, but what I wanted to talk to you about is connected to this. It's about me." I told him I felt I had fallen in love, with whom, and that the feelings were mutual. I told him I had no idea what to do.

There was back story. While training to be a therapist, I had come to know gay and lesbian students and mentors who were comfortable in their identity. I noticed that my way of being in my body and in the world seemed more gay than straight. I shared my thoughts with my husband, and we came to agree that probably I wasn't straight, and that's why our sexual connection was low-key. But nothing changed on account of this conversation except a firming up of our separate identities. We were happy to stay married and parent our kids together. I really didn't want to mess up my life and my family's life.

But now five years later here I was, having fallen in love, which was nothing like the hypothetical possibility of being attracted to women. Nigel said simply, "I think you need to go with this. You need to find out who you are." I had brought my anxiety and conflict about being wrong, and he changed the focus to exploration and learning, a wise and generous move on his part, and a shift that eased my spirit. We agreed that I would take it slowly and keep him informed.

Tea-time meetings with my new love (was she my new love?) became heavy with the burdens of making meaning and making decisions. Neither of us wanted to have an affair. If we were to go forward with this, it would be into the world as partners. I told her about my conversation with my husband. Mary had realized that for many reasons there was no hope for her marriage, and she decided to move from her family home to a condo. Friends helped her move, and I wasn't one of them. "This is about me, not you or us," she said. "I'm really happy just to live there without him." She never wavered in wanting to be with me, but she also never wavered in her care to apply no pressure, to have no expectations of me. She wanted me to be free to choose.

But could I be free to choose? Was this love or was this transference? "I know what I feel for clients, what I felt for you as a client," she said. "This is completely different for me. I'm here as me, all of me. I love you as a person in my life."

"People will say it's an abuse of power. That you're taking advantage."

"I don't care what people say. But it has to feel right to you. Do you feel like I'm still your therapist in some way, that I have some power over you? That I'm taking advantage of that power?"

I thought I saw Mary as a real person, even allowing for the blind besottedness of love. I liked the feeling of being peers and colleagues in spite of our age difference. I didn't feel abused or taken advantage of. But I didn't know whether my feelings could be trusted. That was precisely the issue.

Mary truly didn't care what people would say. It was also the case that those in whom she had confided, friends and colleagues of her generation, including the women in her spirituality group, were all simply happy for her self-discovery, such a long time coming. They were pleased to affirm the beauty of love in all its forms.

My colleagues and friends, a generation younger, weren't all so sanguine. I had three separate conversations with friends concerned about the imbalance of power in the relationship. I told each of them that I had thought a lot about the issue and that I felt I was choosing freely. They let it be, having fulfilled their ethical obligation to speak up. They knew (as I did) that if I were not choosing freely, I might be the last to know.

I spoke with more confidence than I possessed. I asked for an hour with a pastoral counsellor who, in his long career as an external trainer in my institute, had taught both Mary and me, years apart. As he listened to my story, a quiet smile came into his eyes. I knew I didn't have to ask him if he thought such love was wrong. But I did have to say that I was afraid that my therapy transference was being carried forward into the relationship.

He answered with a question. "You know, don't you, that transference is a big part of every intimate relationship?" Mmm, yes, I did know that, theoretically. He added, "We don't get to escape it. We always have to work it out."

I sat and thought for a while. "Maybe I'm just afraid," I said. "Like this is a really hot stove, and if I touch it, I'll get burned."

"What if you could just sit down beside it and get warmed up?"

What if. He couldn't tell me what I should do, but he let me know how he saw me and my situation. This was my attempt to get advice from someone wise and responsible who understood my reality. The conversation settled me slightly. But I was still in a terrible muddle about how I saw me, and the question of professional ethics was just one of the questions churning in me about being right or wrong.

During this time of trial relationship, I invited my parents to a therapy session so that we could talk about my sexual orientation – a story I've told in another essay. I was not surprised by the position they had to take, yet I felt a very hard fall from grace. With them and several of my siblings, I was now the daughter or sister who would need patience and prayer. They would hate the sin while loving the sinner.

There weren't many books written before 1990 that supported Christians to be openly and proudly gay. The little library of our new congregation might have held most of them. I read them all more than once. I didn't read them for information, or even to stabilize a wobbly internal moral compass. I read them for company, these gay and lesbian people who knew what it was like to be called a sinner, but who talked about the rightness and joy of being themselves. They brought soothing, calming presence to my shame anxiety.

My deepest anxiety, however, was not about being seen as a sinner, or as a weird second-class citizen in a society that was still broadly homophobic, or as a therapist with bad professional boundaries. My deepest anxiety was about how I would hurt my children if I continued on this path. To live my sexual identity authentically, I wouldn't be able to continue as the same mom I had always been, in the same family we had always had. There would be a real, painful leaving. Nigel was an adult who, in spite of his own loss and grief, could encourage me to become who I was. But my children had no power, no say, in my leaving.

I could imagine no deeper shame than to be a mom who abandoned her kids just to make herself happy. These eyes looking at me were mine alone, and I couldn't bear what I saw. It was too awful to talk about to anyone. I was on my own with this. The only way I could go forward was, first, to allow that this was not a frivolous making myself happy; it was accepting fully who I was, even though there were days I wanted to get out of it. Second, I would do all I could to change the story from abandonment to taking care. Maybe by force of will and wanting, my wrong-doing could be turned into right-doing.

The trial relationship would have looked like an affair from the outside: meetings in times no one would miss, here and there nights or a weekend away. But it was not a secret. My kids knew about the woman in my life. Once Mary came for a visit and we all walked on the beach together. Years later the eldest told me that after that day she was always waiting for the other shoe to drop. It dropped in the fall when their dad and I told them we would officially separate the next summer.

After Nigel was ordained, he was "settled" in a congregation in a small town outside of Toronto. It was a half-time position. That's when he and I began to take turns living with the kids in the house, half a week each. After six months or so, I moved a few blocks away to an apartment just big enough for the kids and me, and we continued the pattern of half a week with each parent. When Nigel wasn't with the kids, he was in the small manse that came with the settlement. When I wasn't with the kids, I was with Mary in her condo. Sometimes she came and spent time with the kids and me in the apartment. On the boxy little TV in that apartment, we saw the Toronto Blue Jays win their first World Series.

A year later, Mary and I moved into a house with enough bedrooms for everyone and space in the basement to renovate for a kids' TV room and extra bathroom. They stayed with us there on alternate full weeks, switching every Sunday evening, until they left home for university or other kinds of growing up and moving on.

Those homes were the physical spaces in which I tried to do the impossible: live with my kids as if nothing had changed between us, as if I were the good responsible mom taking care of them just as I always had. This was, of course, delusional. Because of my actions, they no longer had the home and family in which they had felt safe. I had connection with and allegiance to someone they didn't know and found hard to trust. Every Sunday night I drove them to another home, another parent and step-parent, and left them there for a week. I felt bereft driving home, but I told myself it was good they could be with Nigel and Jean now. I didn't want to imagine the grief and dislocation they might feel every week, having no single home to call their own, no two parents paying attention only to them.

As their mom, I should have imagined their sorrow and anger about their losses, their disorientation following the changes they had to make. I should have invited conversations about how they felt. But I would have had to lead with accountability, not with shame. They needed to feel my desire to ease their pain and make amends, not my desire to make their pain disappear so that I could feel better. This was the danger in saying I was sorry: that my apology would come not from a place of cohesion and respect for them and for myself, but from a place of falling apart into shame, with the unspoken demand that they hold me together. I think I knew that much, that this would be worse than no apology, no talking. I didn't want to ask them to take care of me.

But I asked anyway, unconsciously, because shame governed my internal sense of good self or bad self. I think they understood this, at least unconsciously. They joked about the Guilt Christmases when

I gave too many gifts. They knew what I was doing. I needed to feel myself being the Good Mom so as not to be the Bad Mom, and I needed them to play along. They needed to play along because they needed a mom who wouldn't fall apart. None of this was about what they truly needed. Shame, the underside of narcissism, made me deeply self-centred. I didn't know much about shame then; I just lived it.

Since the first essay in this book, I've been saying that if only people in families would talk honestly about the hurts they suffer with each other, their painful feelings wouldn't have to go into underground vats of chronic shame to contaminate the soil generation after generation. In this essay I have wished aloud that my parents had been able to be open and honest about the conflict between them and about the mistakes they made in parenting. Why does such talking fail to happen? Because in a system of right and wrong based on shame, whether external or internalized shame, doing something wrong or hurtful makes us vulnerable to being obliterated – made completely wrong, seen as rotten to the core.

Thus, at a crucial time in my life and the lives of my children, I was no more able to talk with them about conflict, moral choices, and emotional pain than my parents had been able to talk with me, and for the same reason, a fear of annihilating shame. For a long time now, this has been my regret, my remorse, about what I did in those years. Leaving my kids alone with their feelings was the wrong I did for which I am accountable and must make amends, the relational rupture which has needed repair. It is still being repaired, as I grow in my capacity to be more simply human, fallible, and present.

I won't blame shame as if it were a force, even then, completely beyond me. As a therapist, I knew that kids need help talking about their feelings when divorce ends family life as they have known it. I wanted to believe that Nigel and I were doing such a good job of amicable separation that my kids didn't need such help.

I knew that blended families are incredibly challenging, that there are reasons for the ubiquitous trope of wicked stepmother. Mary was not wicked, but she was very clear that my kids had two good parents and didn't need her to be another. Her own children and grandchildren occupied her parenting mind. She supported me to give my kids whatever I could, but she didn't have much to give them. Yet she expected a lot of them, often things that turned up only as failed expectations: the proper way to say hello in the morning, to join in dinner table conversation, the proper way to remember a birthday, to say thank you for a week at the cottage.

If Mary complained to me about my kids' lapses, I would say that they meant no disrespect, that they were being good kids in the ways they had learned from me and their dad. I didn't want to be in the middle, the enforcer of her wishes. Her many small ways of being queen of the castle didn't bother me, and I didn't think the kids intended to challenge her entitlement. I asked her to be clear with them about the behaviours she wanted. I trusted they would honour her requests and I believed such conversations would be easier for them than random unspoken implications of failure. But she didn't have such talks with them. Asking my kids for what she wanted from them would have made her feel more vulnerable than she could tolerate.

I didn't understand that then. This vulnerability was hidden from me because Mary hid it from herself. Years in therapy had nurtured her connection with her own soft, vulnerable emotions. I felt tenderness toward this feelingful part of herself that seemed to live so comfortably with her personal power. I didn't realize that her mostly gracious ways of wielding power protected her from another kind of vulnerability, a threat still unbearable: that she would feel dismissed or devalued as a person. I don't think she was aware of feeling this peril in the presence of my children or anyone. Her well-modulated outrage or contempt took care of the danger so quickly and efficiently that her sense of self-at-risk never saw the light of day.

Years later, during the first workshop I ever gave on treating chronic shame, Mary said to a friend of mine, "You know, I don't think I have ever been bothered by shame." In the taxonomy of chronic shame that I would come to develop, she would belong not with those of us who fall apart with shame or those of us who dissociate our emotional selves to escape a constant torment of shame; she would belong with those of us who are able to dissociate shame itself – both our experience of threat and our instinctive means of self-protection.

Although I didn't understand much of this during our first years together, I came to feel it: that it would be pointless or dangerous to ask Mary to reflect on parts of herself she didn't want to know about. I don't think she ever knew, for example, how little she liked sharing me, though this was plain to me and my children from the beginning.

I thought that if I tried to talk with her about this, she would push it away with quick retaliation, making me wrong for noticing something that "wasn't true."

So there we were, both of us in our own ways deeply afraid of being made wrong, living with kids who were hurt, angry, and confused about what was happening, and all of us trying to pretend that we were fine; it was all fine. It was a perfect situation in which to make an appointment with a family therapist and insist that we all go together to talk about what was happening. A good therapist would have sussed out our shame immediately, gently moved us away from questions of anyone being right or wrong, and at the very least made safe space for each of the kids to say to each of us what they were feeling, if that's what they wanted to do.

I didn't make that phone call or insist on that intervention, and I could have. I can't know how it would have turned out, but I do know that I didn't give my kids that chance. This was part of how I left them alone with their feelings – I who had been left alone in my feelings and in that space had come to believe that I was not seen or loved and that I didn't matter; I who believed that children can recover from almost any trauma, but they can't recover from not being able to talk about it.

I feel the swampy suck of shame even as I try to write my way through it, that old delusion, like quicksand, that maybe harsh self-blame will make something better. It's good for the kids, and for me too, that I have learned to feel appropriately guilty for my specific failures instead of being overwhelmed by global shame. But I'm not writing a *mea culpa* either, not really. In the end, what I find myself writing is a canticle of grief about being human. Injuries last. Trauma repeats. In spite of our desires and intentions, in our fragilities we hurt those we love. As I write this song of sorrow, I think of the power of love in the universe, full of grief for all our brokenness, from hearts alone with loss to cities bombed to rubble. What power or presence could help us bear our remorse and sorrow? What love could carry us through to recovery and hope?

In those early days, one of the reasons I was not able to deal honestly with any trouble at home was that my new relationship became entangled with an event of professional humiliation, a fall from grace more excruciating for me than what had happened with my family of origin. As I tried to recover, I had to believe my relationship was worth it. It had to be more than good enough, more than a work in progress; it had to be completely right so that I could prove to the eyes in my professional community, too, that I was not wrong.

I will tell the story in broad brushstrokes. The details don't matter anymore. Many of the major players have died.

Mary was chair of an institute alumni committee that decided to bring in two famous feminist therapists for a lecture open to all Toronto therapists. As training director of the institute, I was asked by the committee to develop reflection questions for small break-out groups that would meet between the lecture and a final plenary session. I was also to find group leaders, and registration was so good that I went beyond our usual volunteers. Two older therapists, men who were now colleagues in the new workgroup I shared with Mary, responded to my request for help. One of them had history I didn't know about.

Some years earlier a student in his small training program (now mine, too) had brought a complaint against him, which was heard and managed within the program, not taken outside to a professional body, as it should have been. He admitted to the violation, apologized, and made financial restitution that was accepted by the complainant, who went on to graduate from the program. The day of the lecture, I was told this story very quickly in the break between the small group sessions and the final plenary. The complainant had been present for the lecture, and had told her story to her small group. I was given this information by someone who knew all of it and wanted me to be ready for what was going to happen in the plenary. I didn't doubt the truth of any of it.

In the plenary session, one of the break-out groups spoke up against the event organizers and institute staff for including a known abuser as a facilitator, thus violating the safety of the women participants in a feminist training event. The complaint was read out formally, and comments to it emerged slowly and then gathered steam as microphones were passed around the hall. Mary was on the stage, sitting rigid and silent behind the two famous feminist therapists who stood together at the podium, listening.

I felt outside of my body as I stood to take a microphone and began to speak. I said that I understood that the violation in question had indeed occurred and had been admitted to and dealt with appropriately. Someone asked, "'Appropriately' by whose measure?" Others added that in-house resolutions of violations cannot be trusted. And besides, the issue is not what happened historically, but the violation of safety here and now.

The feminist therapist speakers were asked to give their opinion on the issue. They agreed with the complaint. This was a here-and-now violation of women's safety and it should not have happened.

The plenary session ended soon after, and I don't remember how. Mary must have thanked the speakers and the gathered assembly for being there. Or something. I remember standing shell-shocked as the auditorium emptied. I remember meeting Mary later, as planned, to help drive the two speakers and their luggage to the airport. It was a long, silent trip.

By the next training day, the business of the institute had become the business of damage control in the larger community and of learning as an organization from our mistakes. The institute's board quickly struck a task force for investigation and education, and of course I was not included on it because I was part of the problem. Not only had I invited the abuser to be a facilitator, but I was a partner in his workgroup. This had been common knowledge but now it was suspect. It was also suspicious that the chair of the alumni committee was a partner in his workgroup. Very quickly the fact, known to many of our friends and colleagues, that said committee chair and I were in relationship also became common knowledge, as well as the even more salacious fact (though we had never kept it secret) that once we had been therapist and client. Somehow this all became one big mess that needed to be cleaned up.

In a small group in the morning, I looked people in the eye and did not flinch as I answered their questions: Had Mary been my therapist? For how long? When did we end therapy? When did we become business partners? When did our current relationship begin? Over lunch, I prepared a statement which answered those questions straightforwardly, and in the afternoon I presented it in a meeting of the whole institute training community. I remember the timelines as well as I do now because I made it my business to document them accurately and to share them when asked.

In those days there was no regulatory college for psychotherapists in Ontario with a code of ethics against which my answers could be judged. A province-wide self-governing society of psychotherapists was just in the planning stage, and Mary was a member of the steering committee. Our history never put her influence there in jeopardy or prevented her from becoming one of the society's early presidents.

But over in my teapot there was a tempest, and I had to survive it. I read the articles on feminist ethics, boundaries, and therapist abuse given to the training community by the task force, and I went to my small assigned discussion group on Sunday afternoons, often feeling like Exhibit A, even if my situation did not come up in the group. It was more likely to come up in a large group, or maybe it came up in small groups other than the one I attended.

One evening, to look after the institute's reputation in the larger community, a group meeting was offered to outside interested parties – to other therapists, for example, who had attended the lecture that blew up. The meeting was facilitated by a professional mediator, and we met in a large room, forty or fifty chairs in a circle, on the first floor of a downtown corporate office building.

At some point, somebody raised the question of my inappropriate relationship. Immediately an older woman whom I didn't know burst out with a protest: "For heaven's sake, leave her alone! If something bad happened there, she was the *victim!*" They did leave me alone then, and I was grateful, even though being Mary's victim would have been my shame. That moment sticks in my mind as my only memory of someone speaking up for me, not that I thought anyone should have.

I assumed I was alone. I hear that now, but I didn't notice it then. I didn't even talk to Mary about how hard this was for me. She attended no educational seminars or large group meetings. Her closest friends knew how hurt and angry she was that the two famous therapists had made an immediate and public judgement of wrongdoing, and afterwards refused to have a conversation with her about it. I had no anger to protect me. I had only my shame to tell me that I was alone in my own mess across all parts of my life, and I had to tough it out the best I could. Of course, that kind of isolation just creates more shame, and that's how chronic shame tightens its vise grip on body and soul.

The task force did its work well, and really none of it was about me. As they intended, they modelled both externally and internally the principles of accountability and response-ability that are applicable

when mistakes are made. Members of the community came to understand far more about the practice of feminist ethical principles than
they had before. When the task force finally wrote up a summary of
findings, they concluded that the main fault in the system had been
naivete in the context of new developments in ethical thinking and
standards for psychotherapists.

I was not censured by the board of directors, but I was told that if
I were to continue to work for the institute, I could not work for any
other training program. I accepted the condition. In fact, the program
I had joined as a new young partner had dissolved itself. My colleague
who had become known as the abuser was taken by the complainant
to his self-regulating professional body, and he accepted its discipline.
I continued in part-time private practice in the office space I shared
with that group. Three years later, when I decided to move on from the
training director position, the institute community put on an evening
of farewell for me that was full of love and appreciation. Anyone there
would have thought I had weathered the storm and come out whole
and well on the other side of it.

––––––––––––

I did not, however, get over feeling visibly marked, though I had no
scarlet letter stitched into the shirts I wore. I didn't attend professional training events or conferences. I joined the new self-regulating
Ontario Society of Psychotherapists, but I didn't go to their meetings.
My propensity to shame made me hypersensitive, but it was also true
that if a student or fellow therapist wanted to fault me for any reason,
they could question my integrity, using my story against me. In those
early days it happened often enough to keep me on edge and make me
crave quiet anonymity.

I wasn't wrong to think that at any time it could happen again. Two
summers ago, some thirty years after the storm broke, a long-time
client came into one of our regular sessions troubled, her trust in
me shaken. "A therapist friend of a friend of mine told me that you
married your therapist. Is this true?" I thought she deserved an answer.
And so I told the story one more time, briefly but truthfully.

"Do you think you did the right thing?" she asked, not accusing,
just wondering.

"I don't know," I said.

I think I did a dangerous thing, though we had moved on to be colleagues. I think it's good that there are rules now to protect clients from the danger of their therapist's power, even after therapy is over. It's not a boundary I'd cross now, as a client or therapist.

"Now you'd think that what you did was wrong?"

Now I'd respect the rules, the guardrails my community has put up for really good reasons – for protection for everybody. But it doesn't help me now to try to decide if I was right or wrong back then. Instead, I accept that I did what I did. I try to live it out with integrity.

Her wondering and worry seemed to dissipate, and we moved on.

Back then, those many years ago, the question of right or wrong didn't help me either. Whether right or wrong, who was I? Or where? In what universe of understanding might I claim integrity? I couldn't even think the question clearly, but it ate away at me.

Meanwhile, I kept working as a therapist, and I joined Mary and others on the faculty of a new relational psychotherapy training program. But she must have sensed my malaise. She began to suggest I go back to school to get a PhD. Maybe she thought academic achievement would restore me to myself. I wasn't interested in achievement. But I could imagine the safety and ease of being back in school and the relief of being with people who knew nothing about me. As I warmed to the idea, I began to want to read things that would help me understand where in the world I was. I found a program in philosophy and education that supported creative interdisciplinary thought. I could commit two days a week to it, plus some evenings and weekends. I would do another MA before the PhD, starting over from the very beginning, giving myself all the time I needed to read and to think.

Graduate school might seem like a strange place to try to find one's personal bearings – but having been raised on Christian theology and philosophy, I needed ideas to help me know who I was and what I should do in the world. Ideas that once scaffolded my sense of purpose had for years been slowly crumbling as I dealt with an onslaught of inner emotion. I hadn't been paying attention, and then suddenly I saw that my former structure of meaning had become rubble to me, and I could barely stand steady in the world with my own decisions. I knew what had happened in my therapy and family life, but I hadn't reckoned with the consequences of change throughout all aspects of my being.

For my MA courses, I read about development across the lifespan, that adults can keep growing when they let old certainties open up to new possibilities. I studied theories of change and of the play between rational and emotional meaning-making. I wrote a master's thesis on how the stories we tell create the persons we become – a never-ending intersubjective process. In my early years, I had been taught that the meaning of life has been given to us once and for all. We are simply to take it in, a truth that does not change. Now I could see this very doctrine as a story. And I was living a different story – one about the power of telling stories. But within this story, a problem emerges: Who is to say which stories are true?

This problem would direct my PhD reading. If all truth is constructed, what makes any particular construction reliable? Consensual validation of what's observed may produce reliable scientific truth. But what about constructions that are based on argument, not empirical evidence? Is rationality neutral? Or does "reason" do its own story-telling to benefit the teller? What powers control the stories that construct our social worlds? On what basis can anyone say that one course of action is right and another is wrong? I asked such questions while reading poststructuralist and feminist theories of the 1990s. I could write reams of answers here, but I will try to keep it simple.

Simple is what I needed in the end. My dissertation noted that both poststructuralist pedagogy and relational psychoanalysis debunk the myth of objective, value-free knowledge. In other words, we all have our reasons for what we teach and learn in classrooms, or for what we explore and discover in therapy rooms. Rather than disguise or apologize for our agendas, we need to own them. It matters that our knowledge is grounded in experience and that it's consensually validated whenever possible, but what matters most is whether or not we do our knowing in order to accept ourselves honestly, face the world as it is, and seek to enhance well-being, ease suffering, and prevent harm. To put it most simply, as humans we're not here to be right. We're here first of all to be fair and good to each other and to ourselves. That's the purpose our knowledge should serve.

I called my dissertation *Thriving on Difficult Knowledge*. Children and adolescents learn about war, racism, poverty, and ecological destruction. People in therapy learn about their repressed suffering and their disavowed emotions, desires, and motivations. The point of taking in such difficult knowledge isn't just to know it; it's to become able to thrive in the face of what's most difficult – to find in conversation with others the agency and capacity to care about what we've learned, to be changed by it, to be moved to take meaningful action.

It's a strange mind-bending concept, knowing as doing, as one of the activities humans can use to hammer out answers to the never-ending question, *how shall we live together in peace and well-being?* Moral knowing, which includes separating right from wrong, is active here too, in this constantly contested human world. The feminist ethicists I read argued that in the messy complications of the real world, rational moral concepts matter less than the doing of empathy, care, and respect. The humanist and feminist versions of psychotherapy that had re-educated my heart taught me to be present and connected, to try to take care of right relationship, not to try to be right. Any left-brain interpretation of my process was a bonus.

I could indulge myself here and speculate that knowledge as a verb – knowing that is simultaneously many kinds of feeling, doing, and being – is probably more a right-brain than a left-brain phenomenon. But that's a connection between theories I understand now. Then it was enough for me to find a theory – a story – that welcomed me into the difficult knowledge of human suffering and failure, including my own, and also encouraged me to seek to live in peace and well-being in response, extending to others empathy, care, and respect.

In this universe of understanding, I could both admit to fallibility and aspire to integrity, even claim it sometimes. Right does not live somewhere above us on a golden cloud, wrong having been cast into an abyss. Questions of right and wrong are *questions* worked out in human community in the face of real dilemmas: What does justice require of us in this instance? What does response-able relationship ask of us here? If we take this course of action, who benefits and who is harmed? Making contested moral decisions is an element of human struggle none of us gets to escape.

I noticed that the theorists I was reading tended to offer strong answers to moral questions. Whether they identified with third-wave feminism, anti-colonialism, or poststructuralist ethics, they were deeply invested in moral principles. In fact, their theory existed on account of their commitments to justice, care, inclusivity, equality, autonomy, accountability, empathy, respect, and more – the list is long; the words hold powerful meanings for hearts and souls. These theorists did not pretend to neutral knowledge.

I thought of where I had first heard that no knowledge is neutral. It seemed the Christian philosophers I had once wanted to emulate were right about this much at least: all of life is religion. Whatever we think or do is based on our heart's commitment, conscious or unconscious. Even when we claim neutrality, denying, for example, any responsibility for systemic oppression, we've made a choice about what we see, believe, and care about. Whether it be our cultural tradition, the light of reason, emancipatory theorizing, the gospel of prosperity, or activism for social justice, we have to serve something, somebody. After all the changes in how I knew myself, I still believed this was true. I was willing to sign on to a set of heart commitments to justice and care, this "religion." I felt inoculated against the virus that can infect any religion: a self-righteous, judgemental othering of anyone whose beliefs do not line up with ours.

Five years after I returned to school, I defended my dissertation and received my degree. I had discovered a universe of thought and belief in which there is no shame in being a fallible, striving human being, where discerning right from wrong is everyday work shared with other fallible people committed to being honest, fair, and kind. I had learned language that would help me develop a moral compass that I could understand from the inside out. In this world of passionately held ideas, I was far from alone. And yet I still felt alone with a trouble that had no name.

I didn't wait five years and then ask myself, "Do you feel better now?" In fact, I did feel better in some ways. I was satisfied to have done good work for its own sake, not to perform "smart." I had developed sturdy new scaffolding for my sense of intellectual and ethical self in the world. Though it was still under construction, it would support more growth and development. Nevertheless, it was only scaffolding. I had known this all along. My nameless trouble ran much deeper, and all along I had been attending to it in another way.

I had gone back to school still shaken to the core by all my falling from grace. My humiliating loss of face in my community had called up negative feelings about myself that I had never been able to bury well. These were two powerful kinds of shame, acute and chronic, but I didn't know that then. They merged into a constant drone of anxious self-recrimination that I couldn't shut off or put into words. This was what brought me to consult the psychoanalyst who told me that he wouldn't work with me because I wanted forgiveness, not analysis. He was perceptive; I was indeed troubled by a being-wrong that felt deeper than thought and beyond argument. But it was also beyond forgiveness. If analysis could help me, it would have to take seriously my conviction that I was deeply wrong in myself.

I was not an analyst myself, but I practiced a psychoanalytic kind of psychotherapy. My first mentors, Winnicott, Fairbairn, and Guntrip, were known as the British Independents, but their theory that put relationship at the centre of human development, pathology, and healing was called "object relations" – *objects* an arcane, rather counterintuitive term for the internal images of significant others that we carry through life. Not many decades later, an American group of analysts centred in Chicago and led by Heinz Kohut had taken object relations ideas in new directions.[1] They called their school of psychoanalysis "self psychology."

Self psychology tells how a self becomes coherent, enlivened, and sturdy through its relationships with its "objects" (powerful external/internal significant others). A young self's connections with its objects are so intense that in early development these objects are experienced as part of self – or "selfobjects." In psychoanalysis, a patient's positive transference to the analyst can reawaken archaic (young) selfobject connectedness that will activate new growth and vitality within the patient's adult self.

I found the language of self psychology a bit off-putting, but I discovered that its nonjudgmental, empathic mode of doing therapy was easily tailored to the needs of my weekly psychotherapy clients. In the safety of our connection, my clients began to experience themselves as more coherent, competent, and worthy of love. Could the same thing happen for my sense of self? Despite all my years in therapy, my sense of self was on the ropes.

I knew that self psychology was designed to address such trouble directly and in all its many versions: selves who feel burdened, shaky, fragmented, weak, flawed or failing, selves living in everyday states of ongoing deficit. To people suffering such self-trouble, self psychology offers nothing more or less than sustained empathic inquiry – in everyday language, a conversation free of judgement or interpretation from the outside in, a conversation quietly insistent on learning, from the inside out, "What's it like to be you?" and following that question as far as it will go.

After the first psychoanalyst had found me wanting, I contacted a self psychological analyst who was indeed a much better fit for me. His consistent empathy created a calm, low-key therapeutic space. It didn't arouse in me the desire for intense connection that had been part of my previous therapies. I slowly moved from seeing this analyst once a week to twice and then three times a week, which led to a different kind of intensity, an ongoing conversation always in the back of my mind and often at the front.

Being understood in the minutiae of my experiences, thoughts, and emotions did help consolidate my sense of self. Talking through the recent experiences that had caused me shame allowed me to stabilize and re-enter my communities. I became able to negotiate my needs more clearly with colleagues, friends, and family. I had someone to talk to about parenting teens and young adults. I discovered more of what I really wanted to say in my writing and my teaching.

All of this was strengthening and sustaining, but I never came into an analytic session and felt at ease. I always felt awkward as I searched for how I would begin. I always left sessions feeling understood but also strangely alone. As other issues settled, I became more aware of my discomfort in my analyst's presence, but I didn't recognize it as shame because his responses to me were never shaming. In fact, I counted on the equanimity of his understanding to support my internal balance.

The shame was mine and always had been. All unaware, I was using analysis to compartmentalize and quiet the shame in my life so that I could do a better job of burying what was chronic and untouchable. But the therapeutic process would ask for more from me. Something about my analyst's way of being with me would call up into our relationship this most distressing part of my self experience, my demoralizing chronic shame.

This fateful repetition, transference as access to the unconscious, is built into the analytic enterprise. I believed this as a general principle, but of course I didn't see it coming. I wasn't supposed to. I was supposed to just find myself in the déjà vu, feel the shock and misery of it, and come to understand it afterwards. That's how the process works. You don't have to like it.

This will be my third account of this experience. This time I'm thinking about what happens when an internalized shaming system has made being right or being wrong the primary markers of our worth. Deciding on right or wrong becomes not only our alignment with truth, but our way to try to resolve interpersonal difficulty. When something bad happens, somebody has to be at fault, either ourselves or the other.

In my first account of the rupture with my analyst, I took the blame. An upsurge of negative transference, my repeating with my analyst a pattern of early emotional distress, uncovered something in me that had been wrong for a long time. Something right was salvaged when I used the story to show how one could survive such repetitions and come out the other side more grounded and whole.[2]

I wrote my second account right after I had written my book on chronic shame. I tried to be fair to my analyst and honour the integrity of his approach, but I also blamed him for what happened. I said that the shame I had felt with him so constantly and then acutely was my response to feeling his absence as an emotional self. Right-brain to right-brain connection was missing for me. Though calming and helpful, his empathy felt to me more cognitive than emotional. I argued that a relational, self psychological practice should be built around right-brain attunement and emotional availability, implying that his practice fell short of that goal.[3]

Now I will tell the story again, and I wonder what will happen if I try to take the right and wrong, the "somebody's to blame," out of it.

I will pick up the story where the distress in my life had settled and I became aware of how uncomfortable I felt with my analyst. I imagined he found my way of talking awkward and inarticulate, my concerns petty. I felt that beneath his required response of empathic understanding, he found me rather tiresome, self-centred, and disgusting. I didn't have those words then, but I remember the feeling well. I thought that if he would talk to me a bit more, I might feel better. He understood that thought, but he didn't talk more. I thought that if I came more often, giving positive selfobject transference more of a chance, I might feel better. That didn't help; in fact, my uneasiness intensified. Maybe the problem was sitting across from him and seeing him look at me. I moved to the couch, but I felt more alone there, talking to a grid of acoustic ceiling tiles. Clearly I was moving more deeply into the trouble, but it remained shapeless, nameless.

There was something I couldn't say, and I think it was this:

You don't judge me. You track my thoughts and feelings well. My anxieties and motivations make sense to you. But is there an emotional connection between us? Do I matter to you? (If I don't matter to you, I am ugly and worthless.).

Of course this question had deep roots in my experience of disconnection with my parents, which perhaps made it unspeakable. In the absence of being able to say it, I did something. That's how enactments come to pass in therapy.

Over the years, I had written many letters to therapists, but never one to him. I didn't feel I had access to an emotional space within him where my letter might land. But I brought him something to read anyway, a chapter of the textbook I was working on. I was reaching for a mattering more of the mind than of the heart, but I didn't think that through. I made this move not long before my analyst was to take a holiday, and that makes sense too. My emotional need for connection with him was muted, but it would have been activated by an impending absence.

I gave him my pages at the end of a session. He received them as a matter-of-fact transaction; he would read them when he had a chance and it might be a while. In the absence of affirming warmth from him, and as I stepped out into the cool, clear light of day on the street, I knew what I had done. My request to be read was a needy, childish acting out of my wanting to matter. The next session I asked that he return the chapter without reading it, and he did. When I took my pages away with me, I was alone with my shame, and I finally knew what it was, simply and clearly. I wrote in my journal and later in my textbook that shame is like a bad burn. Now, in my analyst's presence, I felt that burn acutely. As my long history of shame came clear to me, burn felt right, too: the metaphor of skin destroyed, a slow healing process painful to undergo, lasting disfigurement.

In my analysis I lay in silence. I couldn't speak and my analyst waited for my lead. Eventually, after many days of solitary walks and writing to myself, I did speak, and he responded. We talked directly about what had happened between us. I told him what I had felt. My feelings made sense to him. He did not make them – or me – wrong. I felt that the rupture was repaired fairly well. Not long after, I was able to turn the event into material for the textbook I was working on.

That's all the story I have to tell this time, and I find that interesting. Blame has evaporated. We had our differences of personality, gender, age, training, and ways of thinking and talking. We met across those differences, each of us doing our best in the roles we had assumed to treat my malaise. It was an interaction of good faith, of trying to get to understanding through misunderstanding – the only way through when understanding is difficult. Here I am, three books later, still learning from what happened! At the time, what I needed most was to feel the depth and power of shame within me, and this is how the learning came to me. I packaged it up as quickly as I could in order to possess it, not be possessed, but I would never unlearn that feeling of burning shame or of the tight, deadened scars left by a history of shame. Now I had a name for that thing I feared could happen again, anytime.

One of the myths about psychodynamic therapy or analysis is that once you have the insight, you're released from the power of the thing you didn't know before. Hardly. Psychoanalytic theory has always emphasized a long process of working through. Now that you have the insight, you can begin to see how this thing has constrained your life, and you can try to be wise enough and brave enough to live beyond its constraints, to change the script.

I didn't have much information about what the thing was, this thing I now knew as shame. For a decade, I read whatever I could find about it, on my own and with colleagues and students. After a while I saw that chronic shame was different from everyday reactive shame. I realized that it wasn't directly traceable to experiences of being humiliated or harshly punished. When I finally understood that the genesis of chronic shame had little to do with systems of discipline or moral development and everything to do with right-brain attachment trauma, I was able to write about it. Writing myself into understanding has given me some wisdom and courage to try to live differently, too. That kind of working-through process continues here and now.

Here and now I'm trying to understand how both internal chronic shame and the shame inflicted by social worlds can construct a life in which the only options are being right or being wrong. Absolute right and absolute wrong depend on absolute truth. I'm challenging the absolutes of that system while also saying, paradoxically, that nothing matters more than to tell good from evil as best we can and to pursue goodness. I don't believe that human goodness can be nurtured and protected in a system of right/wrong and true/false policed by shame. That's because a shame system does not leave us the space or give us the courage to struggle hard for whatever goodness, kindness, integrity, and justice we can find and share down amongst the hard realities of life.

I don't believe that veracity is the point of making meaning. We will never have a God's eye view of the truth. In process theology, not even God has such a view. The point of making meaning is less in the provisional truths we come to than in the process itself, when such meaning-making is undertaken in human communities committed to mutual care and respect, to ongoing conversation and negotiation.

I don't believe that being right is the point of being moral or ethical. The point is to do good, to do no harm, and if we find ourselves having done harm, to be accountable and to attend to healing and reparation. The point is to do this in communities of mutual support and accountability, which are not the same as communities of being-right.

Many before me have said things like this, and in many different ways. I'm not writing moral philosophy. Or process theology. I've allowed myself to do some teaching about a therapeutic understanding of chronic shame because I've found that this is often received as new and useful information. It's also what I do for a living, and a leopard can't change her spots. But in truth, what I am writing are just essays, in the spirit of Montaigne, who seems to have invented the form. What he meant by *essais*, however, was simply "attempts" – tries at speaking his mind.

I find it somewhat remarkable, given my history of shame, that I have enough mind of my own to try to speak it. Well, okay; *finally*. I'm seventy. But I don't think I'm done; more on that in the next and final essay.

Here I would like to say, and so I will say, that I'm a better person now – marked by mistakes, sad about failures, owning fragilities, seeking to be kind, and working to be just present and available – than I ever was when I was trying so hard to be right. I like how this state feels.

If only I could travel back in time to share it with my earnest young parents. Within this state of being, they lift their heads and straighten their spines. Their tight shoulders drop and their eyes brighten as they stop trying so hard to be right all day, every day. Instead, they totally enjoy their connected times and also talk openly about what happens when things go awry. They get stressed, angry, and even hurtful, but as soon as they notice, they say that they're sorry, that they'll try to do better. They smile at each other with softness in their eyes because that's how life is: getting hurt and feeling better, failing and fixing, losing and finding one another again. They can manage; it's okay. My small self likes how this state of okay feels. I can grow up safely here, saying sorry when I need to and learning to be kind and fair in spite of my failures.

But time as I know it runs in only one direction. My parents will live out their days seeking to be right in the eyes of God and asking God to forgive their wrongs. My brothers and sisters and I will each develop a moral compass of our own. We will mask our propensities to be somewhat earnest and worried. We will know in our bones, however, that life is meaningful and we're here for a reason. We will all seek grace.

We will each find grace differently. I'm glad to have come to a state that eases my worried spirit. I think it might feel like grace – if grace can be not only an unexpected gift, freely given, but also a feeling. The feeling of grace wouldn't be the opposite of the feeling of shame, something right to wipe out wrong. A feeling of grace would be strong enough to hold shame quietly until it settles into its rightful needing and vulnerable place. That's the kind of forgiveness that matters to me: the kind that makes me not right, but whole.

NOTES

1 For a history of how object relations led to self psychology, including summaries of the thought of Fairbairn, Guntrip, Winnicott, and Kohut, see Howard Bacal and Kenneth Newman, *Theories of Object Relations: Bridges to Self Psychology* (New York: Columbia University Press, 1990).

2 Patricia DeYoung, "The Terribly Hard Part of Relational Psychotherapy," in *Relational Psychotherapy: A Primer* (New York: Routledge, 2003), 133–161.

3 Patricia DeYoung, "Twelve Years Later," in *Relational Psychotherapy: A Primer*, 2nd ed. (New York: Routledge, 2015), 172–208.

REFERENCES

Bacal, Howard, and Kenneth Newman. *Theories of Object Relations: Bridges to Self Psychology*. New York: Columbia University Press, 1990.

DeYoung, Patricia. "The Terribly Hard Part of Relational Psychotherapy." In *Relational Psychotherapy: A Primer*, 133–161. New York: Routledge, 2003.

DeYoung, Patricia. "Twelve Years Later." In *Relational Psychotherapy: A Primer*, 2nd ed., 172–208. New York: Routledge, 2015.

Essay Six

Forty years ago, while thinking about becoming a therapist, I saw the film *Everybody Rides the Carousel*, an animation of Erik Erikson's theory of human psychosocial development.[1] He envisioned life in stages, each of them asking us to meet a specific psychological challenge. Getting old arrives as the question, "Has my life been satisfying, meaningful?" The answer we can hope to find is a felt sense of ego-integrity. The alternative is despair.[2]

In the film, Integrity and Despair are two different old couples. The Integrity couple chats comfortably as they look forward to giving out Halloween candy. One of them makes a gentle joke about getting ready for Death to come knocking. The other responds, "I'm ready for him sometime, but I'm not ready for him now."

The Despair couple holds up a cafeteria line as they fuss about their choices, and then they sit down to bicker. It's clear that this is just what they do. There's no pleasure or hope in the life they share, just meaningless conflict. Only Death will end their squabble, but they don't think about that either.

In broad strokes, the film suggests that integrity in old age looks like being open, kind, and generous in relationship, mindful of the passage of time and life, happy to still have things to enjoy and to give. Despair looks like being locked into a quarrel with others and with life itself, having nothing to give, nothing to enjoy.

Forty years ago, I didn't really think I'd get old one day. But I wondered how I had been meeting the challenges of Erikson's stages. In infancy, had I developed trust, not mistrust? Had my toddler sense of autonomy won out over shame and doubt? My early marks were low, I figured, but they came up when I went to school, where taking initiative and being industrious kept me from feeling guilty and inferior. The identity I had constructed amidst the confusion of adolescence was strong on achievement and weak on emotional coherence, but it

DOI: 10.4324/9781003499121-6

had been enough to take me from isolation into an intimate partner-ship. And as to Erikson's adult "generativity" – I was now parenting three kids and retraining for a productive career. As long as I didn't fall into stagnation in mid-life, it seemed I'd be on track to arrive at old age with a good chance at ego-integrity, not despair.

I'm not so keen on Erikson's stages now. The theory fails to recog-nize the vast diversity of what's "human" in development, based as it is on the psychosocial trajectory of an able-bodied, middle-class, white, straight, cis-gender American male in the 1950s. It also assumes that development happens as a linear sequence of phases. But in fact we're all constantly reworking patterns of being a self while being with others. If relationship teaches us something new about trust, for example, what we've learned about autonomy or intimacy can unravel and reconfigure itself. This dynamic, interactive, iterative process of human development is very hard to map. And that's before we begin to reckon with how relational trauma affects it.

Erikson wrote about "normal" psychosocial human development, assuming that what wasn't deemed normal was mental illness, a common mode of thought in his day. Carl Rogers, however, would soon begin to speak in everyday, non-medical terms about the diffi-culties of becoming a person.[3] The British Independents had started to link such difficulties, which show up as mental disturbance, with traumatic early relationships. Not long after, self psychologists began to describe the kinds of responsiveness infants and children need to become whole and well, and the damage we see in adults who have suffered mostly other kinds of interactions. Instead of enjoying healthy narcissism, they struggle with a sense of self that feels wounded, fra-gile, or fragmented. This sense of a failing self isn't just damage done or an inert deficit; it takes on a life of its own, which I call chronic shame. It's a silent presence in many otherwise functional lives, smudging out bright lines between mental wellness and illness.

Relational trauma makes mapping human psychosocial development very complex indeed. If we read chronic shame into Erikson's story-line, we can see it affecting development from one generation to the next. Anxious shame pulls parents away from caring presence, leaving infants mistrustful and toddlers unsure of their powers. Self-doubt dampens children's initiative and industry. Shame undermines the formation of adolescents' identities, complicates adults' capacities for intimacy, and distracts another generation of parents from what their children need. The cycle repeats. The spin of time dumps older people out into isolated spaces and alienated behaviours that conceal inner battles with shame they've never been able to resolve.

This is the part of the developmental story that matters to me here, the reason I began the essay with Erikson. Getting old is happening to me – a surprise, though it shouldn't be. I remember those old people in the film so very well, especially the bitter, bickering couple. I don't want their last years of despair. I want a felt sense of inner integrity. That's been difficult for me to find, and Erikson couldn't have told me the reason, namely, that relational trauma and chronic shame wreak havoc with anyone's chances, at any time of life, to feel coherent and whole. That's my story and in these essays it's old news now.

There are some new thoughts I want to add, my concerns becoming more existential and ethical as I get older. I'm pondering how chronic shame is related to the core of the human condition, which becomes more undeniable as we age. As the old story tells it, when we're thrown into a world of good and evil, we become ashamed of our naked fragility. We're given fig leaves for cover, but it's hard for us simply to accept the gift. It seems to be in our nature to refuse humility and grab for all the cover and power we can get, driving shame underground where it can't be cared for. I'm wondering whether we could let the vulnerability of ageing invite us to give up our proud refusals. Could we return to the simple shame and need that, when recognized and met, would heal us and bring us peace?

We can be broken and hurt, and we will die. How can we live with this knowledge, especially as we age? We need to believe that our being matters, that when we die, our life will have mattered. Those of us who contend with chronic shame have profound trouble with this issue of mattering. But along with the trouble comes a gift. We've had to search for what we're missing. We have battled to matter. We have put on very fine performances to sometimes great acclaim, and we can tell you that all such mattering is hollow.

We can tell you from the inside that chronic shame floods in to fill the hollowness of emotional disconnection. What has failed us is not our capacity to do but our capacity to be-with. Why couldn't we be-with? Because we were so deathly afraid of being hurt in our places of most vulnerable need.

We learned to be deeply fearful when bad things happened to us long ago. And we're here to tell you, if you suffer from such fear, that you can learn other things now – if you start by feeling vulnerable with people you trust. That's how you'll come to feel held in loving relationship. That's how you'll come to feel like you matter. These feelings happen not in stages, one after the other. They happen slowly, all at the same time, interwoven. Slowly but surely.

Speaking just for myself, I'm grateful that I won't have to wait until the end of my life to feel some of this. An inner sense that I matter is indeed coming to me by way of feeling myself present in the giving and receiving of love. Feeling cherished and valued in my vulnerability is what will hold me together as a coherent self. Whatever "ego-integrity" I come to will be an inclusive wholeness, not a conquering of despair.

Once I might have said that if I can't come through to an integrated sense of self, I'll be left with a self in fragments and shame. Now I would rather say that my more integrated self can't exist without my fragments and shame. They need to matter, too, forever parts of me. Integration isn't resolution. I'm making peace with myself as I make peace with knowing that all of us live in a never-ending tension between rupture and repair, harm and healing. If that's so, I belong with you here. We're in this together, always vulnerable to shame, always needing grace. When I'm knowing that, I can actually *feel* the connection that often eludes me, the loving and the being loved that's here for me.

In Erikson's story of development, all our previous selves have brought us through to the older self we've become. I would add that all those selves are still around. Dynamic, iterative development is still happening as our older self engages with our younger selves. If those relationships are mutually accepting, our older self can rest in a sense of wholeness. If those relationships are mutually demeaning, our older self will struggle hard to feel okay, inner bickering among our disgruntled parts becoming cantankerous irritation with the world.

Those younger selves don't emerge and then disappear with developmental stages. They perform crucial functions at certain times of life and then quietly continue those functions as necessary. If chronic shame is a big problem for us, for example, many of our younger selves will be tangled up with it – some in hiding, still crushed by shame, some relentlessly shaming us in hopes of fixing us, some doing all they can to shut shame out. These selves hold for us the delicate balance of inner self protection we need in order to get on with life in spite of shame.

I'm indebted to Internal Family Systems theory for teaching me to understand internal selves ("parts") by what they each do for the self system they maintain.[4] The IFS way of engaging with these parts as persons invites and nudges the system to work better – as when long-estranged members of a family can start to hear one another and get along better for everyone's benefit.

IFS uses the term *exiles* for the parts of self, often young, who hold the vulnerability of our unmet longings for love. We put them out of our minds because their pain undermines our whole system. Keeping exiles banished is a job for various *protectors*. Some of them are competent adults who create an external life that can be highly successful. If the banished pain starts to break through, however, other kinds of protectors spring to the rescue. IFS calls them *firefighters*. The emergency strategies they use may put our health or relationships at risk, but they are heedless of the mess they make. All that matters to them is putting out the fires of feeling too much.

The most important thing to know about all of these parts is that none of them is bad.[5] The exiles are in pain because something happened to them, not because they are bad, and we can hope they come to know this one day. Protectors' behaviours sometimes cause harm, and we stand accountable. But shame or punishment won't force them to change. What might help is to ask them with sincere curiosity, "Who or what were you trying to protect when you did that?" We're telling them that we don't see them as bad, but as trying to take care. If we listen well and they feel understood in their anxiety and intentions, they might of their own accord find less rigid or harmful ways to protect us from threatened pain.

We can hope that our question comes from a place of grounded, reflective accountability, not from an anxious need to manage or control. In IFS language, our hope is that we speak from a capital-s *Self* who is not entangled or "blended" with the fears and obsessions of one or more of our protector parts. Often it can be hard to tell who speaks because our protectors are so used to running the show and wearing any disguise that works. But if we can, indeed, give Self a voice, we might also tell our various protectors that the exiles in pain are actually our responsibility, and we're finally around to take care of them; would they back off and give us a chance? We might suggest that a certain protector stick around to witness our attempt to make contact with an exile they've banished.

The exile may not be able to speak or even look at us, but we can tell them gently that we're sorry we've not been around all this time. We can say that we're their person now. We'd like to hear what's happened to them, what they need and feel, and nothing they say will be too much for us. But only if they want to, only when they're ready.

Who is this Self who's been missing in action but is now stepping up to shift the balance in this system? In other psychodynamic models we might speak of an observing ego or a coherent, reflective self. This observing, reflecting function is often missing for people who have had to survive relational trauma. That's because none of us can learn to reflect on our own inner process without a caregiver who is consistently in that process with us, holding our mind in mind, helping us to sense and to speak desires, needs, and emotions. Relational trauma is (among other things) the absence of such caregiving.

The capacity for becoming a reflective, coherent self remains within us, however, even when there's no one nearby to activate it. We go searching. Is there a grandparent or an aunt who sees us? What can we learn from friends, from novels, from TV and movies? Maybe a girl-friend or partner can show us how to understand our own mind and emotions. If we're really stuck, we find a therapist. Slowly, slowly, a self emerges to say, "I'm here. I remember. I feel. I choose."

According to IFS theory, this emergent Self can learn to become a creative, compassionate leader of the internal family. With practice, the Self gets better at facilitating conversations that need to happen with exiles and protectors. Mapping who is who and how it all works doesn't change a thing. What matters is being down inside the system, trying to sense what's going on, asking questions and then feeling in turn what each part struggles with, what each part wants, fears, and is trying to manage. The power of change lies in having risky conversations fraught with emotion – parts *feeling* parts – with nobody knowing how the talking will go.

I have done many kinds of psychodynamic work as therapist and as client, and my experience of the IFS model feels to me like another version of that process. Once again, I'm befriending defences so that I can feel my own past and present emotional pain. Once again, compassionate understanding of what I feel alters the patterning of my inner relationships, and thus of my being. Once again, I'm counting on an observer self who can be immersed in all of this, but who can also hold it in heart and mind and continue to make meaning of it going forward.

On the other hand, though I recognize in IFS the deep structure of psychoanalytic theory, I have to say that exploring thoughts and feelings in analysis is nothing like calling out, on a day rife with internal distress, "Hey, what's happening? Can somebody talk to me?" *and having one of my parts answer.* Then we talk, and I find out what the impasse is, who's scared or angry, what set them off. They just need space to be heard. I don't have to do much but be emotionally responsive, genuinely there. What matters is that we're in the same room, talking.

I know better than to ask whether parts are real or not. I have known for decades that transitional space, the space of imagination, illusion, and play (and also of certain therapies), is real. Real things happen there, things that seize your heart and change your life. Winnicott says that both religion and art belong to transitional space.[6] Essays can be written in that space. Right brains are definitely at home there. Having been lonely in that emotional/relational side of my brain for so long, of course I would be keen to discover an internal family there, full of complex emotion I recognize. Of course I would want to grapple hard with those relationships in the improv theatre of my mind.

I'm ready now to begin to tell the last story in this series of essays. You must be thinking that this time I have surely lost the plot. If our topic is shame and getting old, why not just talk about it? It's right there in front of us. As we age, physical indignities multiply, provoking shame at every turn. We can't read fine print or hear quiet conversations. Our hair thins, our skin wrinkles and sags; we manage leaky bladders, bad breath, shaky hands. We begin to lose the strength in our legs and our short-term memory. Arthritic joints seize up. Organs and body systems falter. We take more pills. Who is that tired old person in the mirror? What was that thing I was supposed to do today?

As our bodies slowly fail, we may also lose the engagements that have sustained our minds and spirits. We step back from the demanding, rewarding intensity of work. Travel becomes more difficult. The next generations of family get on with their busy lives without us. Our social circle dwindles as friends lose their abilities to drive, or to walk, or to think. There's less to help us feel whole and well in the face of our ever-more-obvious flaws and failures. Old age is a final test of our ability to metabolize the everyday shame of being less than we would like to be. As always, we will need some help with that.

Our battle with all of this everyday shame is worth talking about. It's the honest context for wondering how on earth we can manage calm, cheerful integrity in old age. But in this essay, I'm more interested in another drama that's played out against this background. It's about shame, too, but chronic shame. I want to explore what happens to it as we age, how the internal deals we've made to disavow or rise above our chronic shame might change as life passes, and what happens to those compensatory patterns when they are assaulted by the everyday losses and indignities of old age.

That's the question I've been setting up here: Is it possible, in old age, to leave behind a lifetime of fragmented states of chronic shame and come through to a sense of self-integrity? My provisional answer: Yes, but the question needs revision. An integrated self will have to include the fragments and the shame; there's no leaving them behind. And how better to embrace fragments of self and their shame than to imagine them living within one's own subjectivity as embattled persons who need to negotiate understanding and peace.

I have my question and a provisional answer, which suggests a direction my story may take. I have my background and stage, and I also have my parts, full of their respective concerns and emotions. There are a couple of key scenes that will matter. But I don't know how it will all come together. Maybe it won't – kind of like the "integrity" of old age. It happens well or not so well. We do what we can and we wait and see.

––––––––––––

Let me begin with a back story of my "parts," a sort of prequel to the story of how we're getting old together. You know these people already, though not as parts. In the first line of the first essay, an eleven-year-old autobiographer says, *Putting your thoughts into writing says that they matter, even thoughts about yourself*. She didn't have much help learning to reflect on her inner world, and already she has a protector part who hides what little she can say. Already she is managing the shame of an icky badness she doesn't understand – but she says what she can.

This nascent Self will have to wait a long time before she's able to feel her inner world and speak it. Yet within the magic of storytelling, her voice is also the voice of a Self who is writing the essay, who at last understands the icky shame and intends to write into its face.

Seen through the lens of parts, the essays begin with childish protectors in place and exiles out of sight and out of mind. There may be one exile or there may be several of different ages, feeling their isolation and despair differently. Where they live, it's dark, and these are the truths they know but can't say: *I am not seen or known. I don't matter. I am not loved. I am not lovable*. As Self, I will say these words for them, and I will hear them.

In the second essay, the one about falling apart, legions of protectors are mobilized to keep it from happening – even though an infant and a small child have already fallen apart alone. We know what has happened, but the protectors are focused on not knowing. Here are some of their names: Obedient Child, Responsible Big Sister, Helpful Daughter, Very Smart Kid, Super Jock, Preacher-Teacher, Reliable Partner, Team Player, Dependable Mom. They perform remarkably well until the bad feelings get through anyway.

Then new kinds of protectors turn up: firefighters who douse emotions with anxious depression, and anti-heroes who have been hiding out in the shadows of goodness and competence. There's a part called Bitter who resents always having to be good and responsible, a part called Lonely who doesn't know how to make friends, and a part called Lost who has no idea how to create a good life in the midst of the hype about being smart and capable. Giving up and turning away from the struggle also protects exiles. That's how the anti-heroes help out.

I (Self) can tell this story now, all those parts jostling to protect their system from feelings they thought would blow it apart. And then it fell apart anyway. I felt some connection and comfort with my children and husband. But mostly I was missing in action, unable to understand what was happening or to take any kind of leadership. Except that I got us to therapy.

In the third essay, "Shame and Relationship," I give some key protectors airtime. It's only fair since they take the brunt of the relationship trouble that chronic shame dumps on us. Right-brain trauma makes it hard for me (or anyone) to be with people easily. I'm learning, but I count on friendly protectors to bridge me across gaps when it's hard. Now I invite Very Smart Kid to explain the link between polyvagal and right-brain theory and make the point that what we can't do isn't our fault. But she wants to say more: "All is not lost! There are at least three reliable, satisfying ways to connect with people even if you can't manage that right-brain, ventral vagal meeting!" She's a bit pedantic, as smart kids tend to be, but she makes a good case.

Then she passes the baton to another friendly protector, Relational Therapist (RT). RT may indeed be the best one of us to describe how chronic shame wrecks intimate relationships and how, in spite of long odds, some couples do find a way back through shamed vulnerability to connection. She has helped them do that, seen it work. Whereas when I step up to talk, I have to admit that I didn't get there in my first marriage, and even now my conflict resolution skills need improvement.

Though I don't go into it, of course my trouble with conflict has roots in my exiles' terror that blame and shame will annihilate them, and in my anti-heroes' prowess at making others wrong so that I don't have to be. In the essay, I let that trouble be what it is, one of the hardest challenges of relationship. Those parts so reactive to shaming conflict will always be with me, one way and another. As the essay moves toward acceptance, not transformation, I ask Preacher-Teacher to say a few words in closing. I stand behind what she has to say: Disavowed shame and hatred will continue to wreak destruction among us, but we can also hold onto hope – if we can keep our hearts open to connection and aligned with love.

I enjoy the camaraderie among these protector parts and myself. I'm grateful for their strengths and insights, and they appreciate my leadership. We've come a long way since the days when, on their own and oblivious to the realities of the situation, my protectors had to keep on producing exceptional achievements while smothering illicit pain.

How did we get here? Essay Four, "Shame and Desire" tells the crucial part of that story: We turned toward the exiles and said, "Tell me what hurts," and we used the relationships of therapy to let their longing, rage, and despair come into protected spaces to be felt. I thought the exiles just needed me to care about what they'd been through. But nourished by understanding, they slowly but surely regained their healthy intensity to connect here and now, to know deeply and to be known. Such forbidden desires became gifts, and I, who had been using therapy to elicit a Self of emotional awareness and agency, had just enough presence to reach out for what was offered.

Just as I had let myself enjoy the gift as given, so, toward the end of the essay, I let myself savour the return of exiled desire, honour my expression of sexuality and gender, and remember dancing at home with the woman I loved. My protectors were all off-stage, silent for the moment, just as they had been when I fell in love so precipitously. Perhaps they'd been in shock then. What I had done was totally off script, terribly dangerous.

My protectors came back with a vengeance in Essay Five, "Shame and Being Right or Wrong." For years, I had asked them in therapy to welcome back parts who'd been exiled for being wrong in ways I hadn't chosen and couldn't help – my messy emotions and desperate needs for connection. Accepting those parts had been hard enough, but this was unthinkable. Since early childhood, my worth had depended on my knowing the difference between right and wrong (as defined by an external, shame-based system) and choosing right. Now my protectors saw me turning toward something blatantly wrong that would get me openly banished, a whole new level of risk.

I felt I was turning toward something hard-won and deeply good for me, though I barely understood my turning. Those protectors who existed specifically to keep us all choosing right, not wrong, felt betrayed, angry, deeply frightened, and totally at sea. I made my choice and then I had to live with their fear and judgement. Maybe I did want their forgiveness. I definitely wanted to feel less torn. I needed a better understanding of ethical responsibility in relation to systems of right and wrong. I sent my Very Smart Kid off to graduate studies in moral philosophy, and I brought the rest of us into a psychoanalysis in which respectful, empathic understanding mattered more than right and wrong.

There, once again, an exile's desire broke through: "Please read what I wrote and respond. (Please show me – with *feeling* – that I matter to you!)" As I saw myself asking, I finally felt my core shame clearly, an inexplicably humiliating desire to be known, felt, and loved. I (Self) was just strong enough to stay with the feeling and bear it. My most fearful protectors wanted nothing to do with any kind of shame, having spent a lifetime battling it. But I kept talking to them. I said that shame was a feeling, not the truth about us. I said we could learn about it together. My Smart Kid started to read about shame; my Teacher started to put shame studies into curriculum.

But my frightened, rigid protectors still accused me harshly of irreparable harm I had done to my three children, as if my admitting to reprehensible moral failure, to being utterly wrong, could make something right. I have been hard-pressed over the years to see those protectors, so caught themselves in right/wrong shaming, as would-be helpers. But I have persisted in talking with them about harm and repair instead of right and wrong, and about what actually helps the people we love. Slowly they have begun to trust another way of feeling better, and I've been able to help the people I love by being accountable for specific harms I've done from a more grounded, integrated place of empathy and desire to repair.

For the rest of my life, I will be having these conversations with parts of myself who learned about right and wrong within the force fields of my parents' anxieties, all of us beneath the judging eyes of God. The fears, beliefs, and desires of those inner protectors and antagonists didn't change when I wrecked the "rightness" of my life. My parts just got rattled, reactive, obstinate, and scared – needing attention, needing conversation.

That would be one way to describe the three decades of my second marriage: constant inner conversation among myself and a crew of inner parts who had thought the world was one way, but then it wasn't. None of us could be told what to think or believe, not even by moral philosophy. We had to find our way together.

Toward the end of the first of our three decades, I was in the psychoanalysis that re-activated a disturbing, shameful longing in me to matter emotionally to my analyst. But at home I didn't have to say, "Please show me – with *feeling* – that I matter to you!" I knew that I was beloved. I could feel Mary's emotional self feeling my emotional self with joy and pleasure. Once, when she told me that her parents had adored her, I thought, "Yes, that's the word for this. She *adores* me." It was a word alien to my experience of family. She also told me that sometimes their adoration missed who she really was and what she really needed. I could sense that edge of being adored, too, but I wasn't about to complain.

In my first marriage, I had carried the weight of Nigel's anxiety. I had made it my responsibility to help him find his way, structure his life, get motivated, believe in himself. It was just what I did, part of our unspoken kinship contract, and I didn't know how wearing it was until I let it go. Mary's life was rich and full of structure. She had no trouble choosing what to do or believing she could do it. The generativity of her adult life had included being a parent, grandparent, therapist, and mentor; maintaining home, office, and cottage properties; building and tending gardens, circles of friends, and communities of colleagues. It was no burden to join forces with her to imagine a new training program or to buy a house. Her father, a doer and builder himself, had believed she could do anything she put her mind to. Now I was living within that cheerful, confident ambience.

And it was more than ambience. It was important to both of us, for different reasons, that we keep our financial affairs separate. When we bought the first house, we drew up a legal agreement that specified our financial obligations to each other, and we set up a joint account to pay for only joint household expenses. But Mary also wanted me to build my own security, and so every birthday she would give me a cheque "to help you max your retirement savings" – a concept new to me.

With her eye for propagating and cultivating, Mary couldn't resist trying to help me realize my potential – which she idealized in an adoring kind of way. I have a photo of the two of us after my PhD convocation. I'm in my gown and new red stole, and she's smiling directly at me. The smile looks pleased as punch and says, "Aren't you wonderful!" I'm looking at the camera, but I know that smile. Mary's idealizing made me squeamish in company; anybody could see it was over the top. Yet in the quiet of our relationship, that proud smile did me a world of good, and I didn't mind that she was gratified to see me flourish.

I started to try new things, not to realize potential, but because I wanted to. I wrote a book; I built a strawbale house in the woods, then sold it to build a cottage on a lake. I wrote curriculum, trained therapists, chaired committees. I bought office space with a friend, renovated it, helped manage the business and community there. I had a full practice, wrote another book, travelled to give lectures and workshops, wrote second editions. This was my life, these were my ventures, my calculations of risk and reward. Mary didn't underwrite them, but she often offered a gift to help and was always available for a start-up or bridge loan.

At my very first book launch, when I said my words to acknowledge the meanings of the event, I thanked Mary with reference to a child's story from a self psychology text: "It's because you're watching me that I can skate." Looking back at thirty years of finding my own strength and generativity in the world, I know that it happened as it did because she always, *always* had my back.

I had not been wrong, those dozen years before the launch, when I had thought that if I could grow up in the presence of a powerful woman, I might learn how to put power and woman together inside myself. This was my side of the narcissistic bond between us, what I needed from Mary to shore up the shakiness of my self-structure. Or as I said to my daughter Adriel once when she asked me why I had chosen this particular person: "I always and forever needed a dad who was safe and secure and a mom who could just love me. The offer of both in one person was too much to walk away from."

I wasn't pleased that this was the truth I could share. I always wished not to need so much, or at least not so visibly – strangers often took us for mother and daughter. But now at least I know that I would have chosen this kind of bond whether or not the chosen partner had once been my therapist. Such transferential projections and narcissistic bonds happen in life just as they do in therapy. Then, as the grandfatherly pastoral counsellor told me those many years ago, we have to work it through.

What was Mary's side of that bond? What does a battleship need, after all? Well, she needed some long-denied emotional/bodily/ sexual intimacy but so did I, and that was an uncomplicated part of our relationship. What was the shaky part of her self-structure that my presence would shore up? This is a tricky question because a battleship, by definition, is not shaky. And yet she definitely needed something.

Mary needed me to go along with her battleship illusion of invulnerability. She needed me not to challenge how she dissociated her own shakiness, shame, and self-doubt. I was to board this sturdy vessel, so to speak, as she sailed it now far from battle under blue skies, charting her own course. She was deeply pleased to be finally master of her own ship, not second to someone who was captain just because he was a man. I was to join her in the satisfying power of the life she lived. Helping me succeed and teaching me to play amplified her pleasure. But I was also to remain myself in my vulnerability, because her exiled parts hiding shame and self-doubt needed me for that. Living with me and loving me, she could know in her bones that scared shakiness can be held and comforted. Her small, frightened parts felt safe with me – even as she denied their existence.

Joining Mary's life was easy. I wasn't attached to things like furniture, carpets, and dinnerware. When my kids needed beds, I assembled IKEA. Since I didn't come with stuff, we lived with hers. I also had no habits of cottage, clubs, or winter holidays. Mary always spent many summer weekends and a full month at the cottage with her kids, grandkids, and friends; now I joined when I could. She reserved the last week of summer for my kids, so we went, of course, all of us falling into her pattern of life.

Early on, the two of us once arranged my sort of holiday for a week in June, planning to cycle in a rural county, staying in various bed-and-breakfasts. Our very first day, Mary spied an advertisement for golf lessons with a pro and a charming nine-hole course overlooking the water. "Come take a lesson," she said. "You'll be good at it." We drove to the course from each B&B we'd booked, and the bikes never came off the rack. I didn't learn to play golf that week, but eventually I did. Soon we were taking golf holidays every winter. I became a regular guest at the golf club and the dinner club, a tourist in a world that wasn't mine.

It was all strange and it was all fine because I was happy enjoying these things with Mary, living in her zone of lucky well-being. I never thought, "Oh, if I had chosen someone else, I could be hiking a rain forest or taking a back-country canoe trip." I was taking care of my basic psychological needs. I wanted to feel connected, safe, and sometimes adored. I didn't care where I ate on a Friday night, and I enjoyed the physical challenge of golf and the long, green walks. If you're shipwrecked and you wash up on a green and pleasant island, you eat the fruit that grows there, no problem.

There was a serious problem, however, in another part of our unspoken deal. I wasn't supposed to notice when Mary's actions came from a place of vulnerability and reactive shame. I was supposed to believe, as she did, that such places did not exist in her. Her anger was always righteous and her reactions always fair. If she felt diminished or vulnerable, the other person was always at fault. I didn't like this pattern for me. I didn't set it off often, but if I did, I worked with it gingerly, reading up on non-violent communication, and starting all my sentences with "I feel …" If I were calm and careful, we might be able to create some middle and meet there, each of us owning some misunderstanding.

I hated this pattern for my adolescent and young adult children, with whom it happened more often. Mary would let herself feel diminished by their small missteps and then blame them for her terribly hurt feelings. She would want me to agree that the kids were as bad as she felt. But I wouldn't agree. She'd believe, then, that I was against her. I'd say no, I just wished she'd have a calm talk with the kid in question; I was only against how her feelings were making the kid all bad. She'd get angrier, saying she had a right to her feelings, and I was denying her that right. These were the worst fights of our life together, the same one bad fight actually, and we never got through it.

Every time I foundered on this fight, I wondered whether I was selling out myself and my kids somehow. I began to see a defensive narcissism in her, as woundable as it was hidden. Was this reactivity the disowned power my friends had warned me about? Was I stuck in a terrible mistake that would cause us both huge pain to exit? Was my own narcissistic neediness ultimately to blame?

Now I can see how a protector part of me got inflamed by her blame and retaliated by making her deeply wrong. (I'm sure I did some of this counter-blaming in our fights, too.) My shamer-protector was also ready to throw me under the bus of being-wrong, along with our whole relationship. But in fact, all the rest of our life together was still there – mutual love and support, generativity and play. And then there was this. What was it? Narcissism is an easy word to throw at it, but it doesn't get to the mystery.

In fact, I don't use narcissism as a pejorative epithet. For me, it's an umbrella term for all the many ways we find to relate to our felt sense of self. Some of us, born into families where recognition and loving presence are easily given, just as easily turn that love toward others – and ourselves as well. Our healthy narcissism is an unselfconscious feeling that we are accepted "as is." Our worthiness is an unthought given.

Others of us, having felt less welcomed and accepted "as is," turn our feelings of being overlooked or rejected inward and worry about our worthiness. Our narcissism is unwell, easily shaken or wounded. We set up our daily lives to get constant reassurance that we are good, valuable, or powerful, and repel anything that might tell us otherwise. This would be "defensive narcissism." I know it well. Usually, I talk about what lies just beneath it, some degree of chronic shame, conscious or unconscious.

Defensive narcissism can be a major or minor theme in our lives. Major or minor, it can blend in well with the strengths and talents of our personalities and emerge only to squelch a breakthrough of some kind of shame. Unfortunately, then the shame never gets worked through, and protective self-with-other patterns get reinforced by this repetition. Such patterns of behaviour can have the auras of battleship, doormat, guru, victim, and all sorts of other things – in IFS language, names or scripts for all kinds of protector parts. My own defensive narcissism tends more toward doormat than battleship, or, from another angle, it doesn't aspire to guru but is often pedantic. Defensive narcissism is not a mystery, though the range of shapes it can take to fit different personalities and lives is amazing. The mystery is what it protects.

For reasons I couldn't fathom, Mary was most reactive with my son, the youngest and most vulnerable of the three kids. Twice when I intervened, she apologized to him, but begrudgingly. Yet years later, nearing her ninetieth birthday, the kids all grown and gone, she told me, "I didn't treat your kids as well as I should have. I wish I had been better to them." I didn't ask her to say more because I didn't think she could. I didn't tell them of her regret. It was one of those things that I wished they could hear from her but I knew she could never say to them. Something was knotted up in her, and pulling at it only tightened the knots.

To put the problem in parts language: When the banishing of a specific vulnerability has been totally successful, we can't even know the name of the exile. I have no idea what disavowed shame made it so hard for Mary to live with stepchildren who thought that her expectations and habits of relationship weren't always wonderful, and sometimes weren't even fair or right. In all the stories I heard of Mary's early years, and there were many, I heard hints of her feeling inadequate and humiliated in amongst feeling needed and adored. There was an expectation of rising above. I could spin a tale, but I won't go there. It wasn't my family. This will remain her mystery.

We all carry such mysteries, and they deserve respect. I don't know anyone who doesn't worry sometimes about their worth or lovability, who doesn't compensate somewhat for shame. This essay isn't about laying bare vulnerability. It's about how we carry the deals we have made with life, our vulnerabilities along with our protections, into our latter days with whatever honesty and grace we can find.

Mary's latter days crept up on her little by little. She chose a time to gift her cottage to her three adult children equally. But this well-intentioned action destroyed the fragile peace that had existed among the four of them. For years she mourned broken relationships and the loss of her happy-family illusion. Rufus, her beloved red poodle, became too old to live without pain, and she let him go. We took our last winter golf holiday; airports and unfamiliar golf courses were too hard, health insurance too steep.

At home Mary kept trying to cook an evening meal a week, but organization got away from her. When I saw her distress, I said I didn't mind doing all the cooking. She was relieved and also began to suggest dinner every Friday at her club as my "break." In 1944, at fifteen, she had joined this club to play badminton; in her eighties she was meeting friends there every Tuesday for lunch and bridge. And then in 2017 it burnt down.

She had another bridge club, a bigger one, which meant more friends. Duplicate bridge kept Mary's mind sharp, her competitive juices flowing, her social circle robust. Younger partners would come to pick her up for the game, the high point of her week. Other friend circles from her high school, university, and therapist days had crumbled away as people died or became infirm. Alone at home, she watched her favourite TV shows; in good weather she took the car and her cane out to the library or the liquor store.

Mary was anxious to have me home with her. I gave up the teaching that had me away some weekends, and I gave up working evenings. Still, when her arthritis was flaring or when she was bored and lonely, she would have had a second martini by the time I got home from work. She wouldn't remember if it was her first or second, but I could tell. This isn't safe, I would say. She would disagree.

I knew what was happening. It was sad. It was inevitable. It was life. There were precious few times in a week when I could feel we were partners. I had become Mary's caregiver. The more I had to be unfailingly kind, reliable, and patient, the less I could be present as myself. I felt guilty about the distance in me. She must have felt my disconnection, and so she would call for me all the more. I would grit myself into more patience. It was a long, slow spiral going nowhere good. And then the pandemic hit, locking us down together, and it didn't work at all, her needing me while I needed to work on video.

I found my solution by renting a small office nearby where I could work without interruption and then get home fast. Personal service workers came in for some of the time I was away. I was happy for their help with Mary's personal care. She had found her solution by going to bed, and not all their cajoling would get her up and out of her pyjamas. They didn't know that they were trying to turn a battleship.

But she would gladly get up and get dressed to go to the lakehouse. So there we were, eighteen months into the pandemic, less locked down. Maybe it was because other people could now feel their freedom returning, maybe it was because the night before, when I'd said I was going to the basement hot tub, she'd said, "Please don't go down there, I'll be scared here alone," but in any case, as I set off to walk the dog on that first morning of our first full day there, I felt I had hit a wall. I thought I might explode.

My being out with the dog didn't scare Mary or make her feel alone; dog-walking she understood as a necessary daily routine. Walking this dog whom we'd adopted in 2019 had been my sanity during lockdown, and now it was my freedom, an hour in the morning, half an hour in the afternoon.

I didn't explode. First I walked hard and fast past all the cottages where people were getting up, having breakfast, going out to the dock. I needed a private stretch of road. When I got there, inside my head I yelled, "What's happening? Can somebody talk to me?" Well, maybe not just inside my head. I don't mind talking to myself when nobody's around. I had done parts work before, but never while walking a dog on a rural road, feeling desperate. Somebody answered, loud and bitter: *I hate this life. I am fucking fed up with it. I've had it. I'm done.* Okay. That felt real. I could take it from there.

Bitter had never spoken up before, though she'd been there ever since she'd tried hard to matter by being Good Daughter and Responsible Sister. *All that hanging diapers, drying dishes, cleaning sinks, ironing, sweeping, and babysitting, and for what? The work isn't the problem. The problem is, I do everything I'm supposed to, no complaining, but I get nothing. When do I get to be seen, cared about? When do I get to matter? I HATE THIS LIFE!*

"Ok," I said.

> I get it. Not mattering sucks. It hurts. You feel that this very same thing is happening right here, right now. You know what? It IS happening right here, right now. We don't matter to her the way we used to. She just needs us. She can't see us anymore. It's true.

Being heard, Bitter went quiet, a bit shocked, a bit calmed. "Anything else?" I asked, fine to continue the conversation.

But there was another voice coming through, also bitter but a lot meaner. It was taking a strip off me. *This is all your own fault. Don't you go crying to anybody. You got yourself into this, you made your bed —HA! — and now you've got to lie in it. You could have seen thirty years ago that this was where it would end. You could have done the math. You thought you knew what you were doing, you thought you were smart. You STUPID, STUPID KID!*

Oh. Ouch. I tried to stay calm and curious. "Anybody have anything to say to that?"

I hate you!

This sounded like yet another voice. I didn't know who was speaking, or to whom, but I had to say something. "You hate me for being stupid?"

No, I'm not talking to you. I'm talking to her, the grown-up. There was a kid, there was a grown-up. I want to tell her,

> You were the grown-up; you could have taken care. I was thirty-seven, for God's sake. A kid. You just wanted me and you took what you

wanted. I hate you for doing this to me, to my kids, to my family. Using me is not love. It was never about me. I don't matter and I never did. I ... hate ... you.

Nobody had anything more to say right then, not even me. I still wasn't sure who had spoken. There was just space all around the thing that had been said, the thing I was never supposed to say, or even think, or feel. Saying it would make it true. And that would be the end of everything.

Except saying it didn't make it true, and it wasn't the end of everything. It was true that somebody felt that way and it was a terrible, terrible feeling. After a while I could say that much: "I understand what you're feeling. It makes sense to me. I know it feels terrible. But it doesn't make you bad."

That wasn't all that happened. I walked for eight mornings and seven afternoons. I wrote out conversations on my computer in the evenings after Mary went to bed. Parts I had known from before came back to me, and new ones turned up. Interactions felt risky and intense, but when they were hardest, space opened up around them.

As the week passed, space came into the house with me as lightness and ease between the two of us. Kind, patient moments happened on their own. I felt the return of a gentle tenderness toward Mary. It was all subtle, quiet, and invisible, this spaciousness, and it was one of the best surprises of my life. Some therapist part of me could have explained it to me, but I didn't want to hear it. I wanted to live surprised by wonder for a while.

All my people, such intensities of feeling, so many layers and relationships, so many conversations still to have! But it was all mine to do. They would speak to me, and they could trust me with the very worst stuff. Nobody was going to die from being real. I had heard some terrible things that I just had to be with – and now I felt better. No, not *better*, exactly. *Different*.

That was the end of August. Late September I was surfing a real estate site, looking at farms not too far from the city. Now and again, I liked to spend some downtime looking at homes and properties, imagining alternate lives. A farm had been on my fantasy wish list for a long time. Now was not the time, but it didn't hurt to dream.

Looking back, I can see that I was imagining spaciousness into the world. That's why I noticed, when I clicked on one farm for sale, that there was a small town up the highway, and in that town there was a seniors' residence. The property wasn't right, but the idea fell into place in my mind fully formed. Mary and I could live in the country together Fridays through Sundays. She could be safe in a residence the four days I worked. I could visit her there, evenings. We would have that safe place for her as she needed more care.

I decided to talk to her about it. It wouldn't be the first time we had talked about moving to the country one day. But never like this. What she wanted now was to live in peace and comfort in her own bed, with me right by her side until she died – which could be years, I knew. In the simplicity of her dementia, she couldn't consider the complications of what she wanted; it would be up to me to make the impossible possible. And I knew that even if I could somehow make it work, she would just need more and more from me, and I would end up hating her again.

I left the idea with her, and by the next day, she had clearly put her mind to it. She wasn't interested in the details. She didn't want to make any decisions. There was one sentence that she said twice, or maybe three times, as if she had practiced it to make sure she'd say just what she meant: *I trust you to do what's best for both of us.*

I heard it as a call to my adult Self to step up. It was time for me to let go of my side of our narcissistic bond. Endlessly doing good without complaint wasn't going to get the kid in me the mattering I needed. I had met Bitter, and I didn't want to live there. I felt Mary's trust to be real, even sacred, which helped me step up. She was letting go of her side of our narcissistic bond. She was concerned for my well-being too, along with her own. She was acknowledging her vulnerability as well as she could, putting it in my hands, consciously giving over control. I would take her at her word and try hard to do what was best for both of us.

By November, I had found the house in the meadow four minutes from the upscale seniors' residence overlooking Georgian Bay. We moved north in the spring, she to "assisted living" in her small room with a view, me to the "farm." We were in the old age of our relationship. This time would be shorter and more fraught and fragile than I had imagined.

The residence was well-appointed, the food good, the staff reliable. But like every such place it ran on a schedule. Mary refused to be put on a schedule. She'd have a shower or get dressed or go to the dining room only if and when she wanted to. The battleship part of her was down to its last strategy.

I had seen the progression of strategies. Her entire life, Mary had known herself as self-motivated and self-directed, competent to set her goals and meet them. In her mid-eighties, some memory loss and physical frailty challenged that sense of self. She became more rigid in her ways and critical of others, battening down the hatches. Then as more competence slipped away, she became more demanding that her needs be met. I saw how she managed, even in neediness, to cling to power – as she'd done at home when she took to her bed.

I understood what Mary was doing now. When I came to visit, late afternoons, I wouldn't mind whether she was in clothes or pyjamas. (In fact, I got her four new sets of classy pyjamas.) I noticed trays of lunch or dinner, eaten or not. Staff thought her dementia made her anti-social, unwilling to come to meals. Yes and no. Mostly she was saying on every front possible, "You can't make me." I didn't try to get Mary to be "good" for them. I'd heat her food if she wanted some. I brought her favourite snacks to share. I mixed up tiny martinis for both of us. We watched TV, listened to music, and talked about all the family photos on her wall, naming people one by one. She was always so very glad to see me and I was always so very glad to see her. It was just us there in her room together, doing as we pleased.

In the midst of all the turmoil of transition and my wondering, "What's best for both of us?", one thing was clear to me. This move would have been worth doing if only for the *feeling* of love that came back between us – a wonderful unexpected gift. When I thought about it, I understood. I could be happy to connect because I could also leave to be free, and she could absorb my happy presence instead of my smothered resentment. Almost every day, for at least a couple of hours, and often without many words, we each felt remembered and treasured by the other.

When Mary landed in the ER in November, the physicians told me they didn't see how she could survive the state of sepsis she was in, but she did, miraculously. She was taken to a ward where they would try to coax her back to health with loads of pills and continual IV drips.

She was catheterized and monitored constantly. She hated being there. She refused to eat. She refused to swallow pills and she pulled IVs out.

I had a conference with her young doctor, who was also a specialist in end-of-life care. "I think she's trying to tell us something," he said. I agreed. "She doesn't want any more interventions." No, she didn't. He said that given her age and the damage to her organs, with continued interventions Mary would probably die anyway, but more slowly. I wondered whether he thought she wanted to die. I didn't think she wanted to die. She wanted to live, but on her terms.

Maybe that's the essence of palliative care, not being helped to die, but being helped to live on your own terms until you die. Luckily, the care in the hospital's palliative unit matched Mary's terms exactly. She could go to bed in peace and be looked after expertly and kindly until the very end. I was sad but also deeply grateful that I could be certain at last that I was doing something that she wanted and something that was best for her.

It's more than a year later now, early Christmas evening. I have been writing most of the day, here alone at the farm. This is where I want to be and what I want to be doing. My family wishes me well. I will see them soon. I would like to finish these essays before January 15, which is the first anniversary of Mary's death. Finishing before the end of this year would be even better.

Last year at this time, I had walked down the palliative care hall with gifts: a new orchid plant – Mary now called them "the flowers with faces" – and an azalea, bright red in honour of the day. Flowers, especially orchids, always made her happy. She asked me to check all her plants to see if they were dry. One or two needed watering, so I gave them a drink. Outside the window, the lights of hospital rooms lit patches of new snow between the trunks of birches.

In the cupboard beside the window, there were the handmade shortbread cookies her daughter Madeleine had left for us. I put one for Mary and one for me on napkins on her rolling tray. I poured two small glasses of rye and water on the "rocks" – pebbles of hospital ice. I knew that at best she would lick or nibble the cookie, and that although she loved the look of a fresh drink, and might take a taste, she was beyond drinking it. But still we needed the ritual of something to eat and to drink together on this Christmas evening. I took my time setting up the ritual, since that's what mattered.

I started the playlist of Christmas music I had made for us, hymns and carols one would know from having grown up in church, as we both had. It was bearable, not grocery store. I kept the volume low. And then I sat down and pulled up my chair close to the cookies and the drinks.

"Cheers!" Mary smiled, and lifted her drink an inch.

"Cheers! And Merry Christmas, My Love," I said.

"It's Christmas! That's right!" she remembered. (I had said so once or twice already.) "You brought me flowers. Thank you, Sweetie." (She had thanked me once or twice already.)

"Yes, I did bring flowers. You're welcome. And I get to enjoy them, too!" We looked at the plants and flowers and talked about them one by one. Then I pointed to the big photo of Rufus on the wall, all floppy ears and bright eyes. "Remember Rufus and the Christmas stockings? He knew about the cashews, didn't he?"

"Oh, yes, Rufus loved his cashews! As soon as it was Christmas morning, he knew! He'd come running down the stairs!" We laughed. It was always a favourite memory, right there to be taken out and polished up.

Mary frowned. "Oh, but I want to give you a present. You must need some money. I have plenty of money, you know!"

(Oh, my little battleship!) "Yes, you do have plenty of money. But I don't need any money. I have everything I need. And do you know why? Because for all these years you have been so good to me. You have already taken care of me so well." I didn't want to cry because tears confused her now.

I managed a quiet chuckle instead. "You'll just have to love me for Christmas. I'd like that. We can love each other for Christmas, how's that for a plan?"

She smiled back at me, pleased to play along with my gentle banter. "That's a good plan."

"What do you think of the music?" I asked. She wrinkled up her nose. "Yeah, me too. Boring, right? Shall we switch to something you like better?"

She decided she wanted to lie back in the bed and listen to her favourite playlist. Our little party was over. I tidied up the tray and then pulled my chair around to where I usually sat, where I could manage the music and hold her hand. Already her eyes were closed, but she smiled when it began, cello and piano.

I took her hand as always, and the music washed over us. I imagined that it helped her feel alive and calm, held and whole. It had become a meditative practice for me, connecting to her and to myself, the music as soundtrack. An hour or more every night to keep me calm and whole. When it ended, she was fast asleep, but I kissed her good-night anyway.

What do I have to say about shame and old age now?

In the old age of our relationship, we did no final working through of our deficiencies and defences to arrive at integrated maturity. But we were given chances to be present to what we could bear of our own need and shame. We had time to listen to what Death had to say: *This will be over soon. Think about what matters.* We found ways to allow that all the bruised, fractious, stubborn parts of us needed to be loved.

Without being put into words or even brought to conscious awareness, this quiet accepting of what was real became part of our connection, along with knowing that we didn't have to like all of it. We could just be there with ourselves and with each other. In her last years, dementia eroded Mary's memory and her capacities for complex mental process, but in the grace of our situation, it didn't touch her ability to be simply present and to give and receive love.

As I said early in this essay, my battle with chronic shame has taught me that feeling that I matter depends on feeling that I'm connected, that I'm able to give love and to receive love. None of us should have to wait until we're old for this to come home to us. But getting old does give us some distance on all our striving and achieving, all the work of our hands and minds, time to ponder what has mattered and where our mattering lies now. We still have time to come home to loving and being loved.

And if shame is still getting in the way, now's the time to realize that we need to bring shame home with us. Ageing may rob us of our dignity and make us face our final vulnerability, but it also asks us to stop pretending that we're other than we are. It asks us to be present and honest, to make amends, to reach out with kindness, to accept the care we need, to turn with our shame toward grace.

Being old can be lonely. It can also be a time of knowing that we're all in this together, always vulnerable to shame, always needing grace. When we bring that spirit to the people in our lives, however few they have become or however fragile our connections, we will create space for belonging and love. In that space, they will matter, and we will matter, too.

––––––––––

I know that seventy isn't really old. But I have never been any kind of old before. In all my years with Mary, I was always the young one. Then she died, and I woke up to being on my own and seventy.

Still, this essay is not based on my firsthand knowledge of getting old. I have not suffered many indignities yet. I still work and walk the dog, cook and garden, read and write. I am at the front end of a time in life called old (I can't delay my Canada Pension any longer), but it's come to be divided into young-old, middle-old, and old-old. We young-oldsters can still pretend that we're not getting old, that the pension is an anomaly.

I did have firsthand knowledge of how my relationship with Mary, a part of me, grew very old and then died with her. But wherever this essay is truly about being old, it's based on my being with her in her old-old years. It was not firsthand experience, but it was intimate and powerful. I did not experience all of her frustrations, losses, and humiliations, but I was nearby. I have been to the country of the old-old and the infirm, and not just for a visit. I've been there long enough to know in my bones that unless I die suddenly, I'll find myself living there too, one way or another.

What way will that be? How will I live when I am very old? So much will depend on how I live for the next two decades, if I'm given that time. I choose integration that brings lovingkindness to all the haunted, reactive parts of myself and their shame – and to all my other parts, too. I choose to make time to love and be loved, and to rest easy about mattering.

When I listen to the intensity that I have poured into these essays, I hear grief telling its stories in many colours of memory and ending.

I hear my doggedness to find a new relationship with my shame and with the grace that has been with me all this time. And I hear something else, a little wild and a little free (for me). The power of love in the universe can be wild and free, I hear.

NOTES

1 *Everybody Rides the Carousel*, directed by John Hubley and Faith Hubley (Hubley Studios, 1976), 76 minutes.
2 Erik Erikson, "Eight Ages of Man," in *Childhood and Society* (New York: Norton, 1993), 247–274.
3 Carl Rogers, *On Becoming a Person* (Boston, MA: Houghton-Mifflin, 1961).
4 Richard Schwartz and Martha Sweezy, *Internal Family Systems Therapy*, 2nd ed. (New York: Guilford, 2020).
5 Richard Schwartz, *No Bad Parts: Healing Trauma and Restoring Wholeness with the Internal Family Systems Model* (Boulder, CO: Sounds True, 2021).
6 Donald W. Winnicott, "Transitional Objects and Transitional Phenomena," in *Playing and Reality* (New York: Routledge, 1989), 1–25.

REFERENCES

Erikson, Erik. "Eight Ages of Man." In *Childhood and Society*, 247–274. New York: Norton, 1993.
Hubley, John, and Faith Hubley. *Everybody Rides the Carousel*. Hubley Studios, 1976. 76 minutes. https://vivostream.fiu.edu/player/v1/embed-video.html?48427add-b34e-4691-9b44-aae041596beb
Rogers, Carl. *On Becoming a Person*. Boston, MA: Houghton-Mifflin, 1961.
Schwartz, Richard. *No Bad Parts: Healing Trauma and Restoring Wholeness with the Internal Family Systems Model*. Boulder, CO: Sounds True, 2021.
Schwartz, Richard, and Martha Sweezy. *Internal Family Systems Therapy*, 2nd ed. New York: Guilford, 2020.
Winnicott, Donald W. "Transitional Objects and Transitional Phenomena." In *Playing and Reality*, 1–25. New York: Routledge, 1989.

Index

Note: Page numbers followed by "n" denote endnotes.

intimacy: adults' capacities for 136–137; bodily 148; emotional 69, 76, 148; sexual 148; *see also* love; relationships

Judeo-Christian myth 78
justice 17–18, 21, 45–46, 132; reparative 80; social 64, 126

kindness 18, 65, 67, 74, 76, 81, 83, 132, 161
Kohut, Heinz 127, 134n1

Little House (Ingalls Wilder) 24
love 9–12, 15–21, 49, 53, 67–70, 78, 80–82, 110–113

Michigan 4, 6, 10–11, 43
momentary shame 30
Montaigne, Michel de 132
moral: agency 108–109; compass 109, 113, 126, 133; education 110; knowing 125
motivations 125, 130
multigenerational chronic shame 8, 72
mutual regulation 32

narcissism: defensive 150–151; healthy 136, 151
nascent Self 143

object relations 127, 134n1
Oedipal conflict 88, 98–99

palliative care 75, 105, 158
"pastoral care" 60
personal chronic shame 8
polyvagal theory 56–57
Porges, Stephen 55
poststructuralist ethics 126
poststructuralist pedagogy 124
poststructuralist theory 124
poverty 125
predestination 2, 15, 18, 44
process theology 20, 21, 132

protectors 139, 140, 143–146
psychoanalytic psychotherapy 35, 127
psychoanalytic theory 90, 131
psychodynamic therapy 90–91, 131
psychosocial human development 136
psychotherapy 56; demystifying "troubled mind" 56; humanist and feminist versions of 125; psychoanalytic 35, 127; relational 64, 123

racism 125
reactive shame 131, 150
real relationships 89
Reformed or Christian Reformed Churches 2, 10
relational chronic shame 6
relational distress 9
relational psychoanalysis 124
relational psychotherapy 64, 123
Relational Therapist (RT) 144
relational trauma 64, 136, 137, 140
relationships: adult 12; attachment 32, 34, 108; damaged 17; destructive 4; and healing 21; real 89; sexual 111; and shame 55–82; therapeutic 89; trial 113–114; *see also* intimacy; love
reparative justice 80
respect 16, 22, 61, 69, 79–81, 95, 115, 125–126, 132, 152
right brain theory 56, 144
Rogers, Carl 136

same sex desire 103–104, 111
Schore, Allan 32, 35
self-compassion 79
self-integrity 142
selfobject transference 129
self psychology 127–128, 134n1
self psychology theory 96
self/Self: emergent 140; emotional 34–35, 50–51, 56, 94–95, 129, 147; ethical 126; nascent 143
sensual desire 87, 91

Printed in the United States
by Baker & Taylor Publisher Services